Memoirs of a Liverpool Stripper

Florence Jones

Pharaoh Press

Memoirs of a Liverpool Stripper
ISBN 0 9525543 1 3

First Published March 1996 by Pharaoh Press
2nd Edition Reprinted May 1996

Published by Pharaoh Press,
Roby, Liverpool 36.

Produced, printed and bound by

Brunswick Dock, Liverpool, L3 4BD.

Liverpool Skyline from the
C. Hulme Collection, Garston.

Dedication

This book is dedicated to Joy Peach
without whom my memoirs
would have remained untold

Temperance Song

Father dear father
Come home with me now
The clock in the steeple strikes one
You promised, dear father
That you would come home
As soon as your day's work was done.

The fire has gone out
The house is all dark
And mother's been watching since tea
With poor brother Benny
So sick in her arms
And no-one to help her but me.

Please father, dear father come home
The house is still dark and Benny has gone
To the angels above the blue sky
And these were the very last words that he said
'I want to kiss father goodbye'.

Chapter I

"Come on, they're Germans! We don't want them here."

People were shouting and running from the side streets into the main road. There was a sound of glass breaking and I was in the middle of a screaming, jostling stone-throwing mob until my elder brother pushed his way through the crowd, grabbed my hand, and led me home.

In Verona Street where we lived, we passed a shippen belonging to Hargreaves the cowkeeper. The wide gate was open and the big brown cows stood staring out, their jaws slowly moving as they chewed. The cows scared me, especially when they were driven through town from other cowkeepers' places and people had to jump into shop doorways to avoid their lumbering hooves.

I was crying when we walked into the house. "What's Germans?" I asked through my tears.

"What's the matter with her?" my mother said.

"There's a mob stoning the sweetshop in Robson Street. I had to get her out."

"What's Germans?" I persisted.

"They're the enemy. They've been sinking our ships and killing our soldiers."

"Why?"

"Because there's a war on. You're too young to understand."

"No I'm not! I'll soon be five and going to school."

"Don't argue. Go and play in the yard 'til your tea's ready."

Edie was bouncing a ball on a penny on the ground by the wall. "What are you crying for?"

"I'm frightened.

"Yer always frightened."

She was right, I was. She was the ring leader in any mischief we got into. But because I was older, I was always the one to get the blame. She was the baby and knew she wouldn't get told off or sent to bed. That's why I was always frightened.

Our six-roomed house was full of people. Edie and I slept in a single bed in our parents' bedroom, my elder sisters, Harriet (who was called Queenie by everybody) and Dolly were in the middle room, while the boys slept in the small room at the top of the stairs.

Dad was too old to go in the army, the boys were too young. Harriet worked in munitions. Her hands were always yellow with the powder she used in the job.

As each girl went to school, the next one took over and went to market with mother, walking down the hills. When my turn came, I liked going to market because on the way we called on a friend we knew as Aunt Mary. Her mother lived with her, a white-haired old lady who used to give me a sweet or a biscuit.

One day when we called, the old lady was ill in bed. A few

weeks later she was downstairs lying very still.

"She's gone, Harriet," Aunt Mary said to my mother. I was puzzled. She hadn't gone. There she was lying there.

"Touch her," Aunt Mary said.

I did. She was so cold. Even now I remember the coldness. It used to be said that touching a dead person stopped you dreaming about them. It's not true. It wasn't for me anyway.

In the winter, our trip to market was no picnic. With hands frozen, fingers aching with chilblains, we often rested on the Church steps at the top of the hill.

Otherwise shopping was good. Standing in a queue at the Maypole you could watch the assistant plonk a lump of butter onto a slab and with two wooden spatulas slap the butter into a half pound block and then wrap the paper around it ready for the next customer.

We didn't have butter but margarine which was not from the Maypole but other brands we called 'wagon fat'. Shops were always anxious for custom, and you didn't dare go into one shop displaying goods brought from another.

Monday was washing day. All the things from the Pembroke table in the back kitchen went onto the table in the kitchen. The huge mangle with wooden rollers took up most of one wall. As we grew older we helped mam to thread the clothes into it or turn the handle.

On wet days the clothes were dried on a rack hauled up near the ceiling by a pulley.

Tuesday was the day for cleaning the brasses. There were a lot of them: a curb, an iron holder, a trivet and a bell. But worst of all a huge brass plate with the inscription:

Mrs Titherington, Certified Midwife

Mrs Titherington was my father's mother. She had had sixteen children of her own. As my mother's people lived in Scotland, the younger ones in the family never knew any grandparents. When she got annoyed, mother's broad Scots accent made it hard for us to understand her.

I hated getting my hands dirty with the Brasso and complained. "It's not fair, the boys don't do anything."

"That's the way it is, so stop grumbling."

"We take the bunloaves." Jack said.

"That's only once a year ..."

But it was no use. They were males. Not like us. Sometimes they were very good to us, letting us ride on the back steps of their bikes, and taking us rowing on Stanley Park lake; giving me a leg-up when the ball went over a backyard wall while we were playing cricket in the entry — but that was because the householder would have shouted at a boy climbing over their wall, but didn't bother if it was a girl as long as she shut the door on her way out again.

The highlight of the week was the children's matinee at the Mere Lane picture house on Saturday. The smaller ones sat on planks at the front, but it was better to sit in the middle, because when a late-comer arrived and stood at the front looking for a place, the doorman would come along and lift the little ones closer together to make room. As soon as he'd gone, the boys pushed so much that it sent the ones at the end of the plank flying into the aisle. If the culprits were caught they'd be thrown out.

Before the picture started, the noise was deafening with the children shouting and throwing orange peel down from the balcony to attract the attention of their mates. If it happened to hit you, the orange peel stung. Once the film started the noise subsided except for the boos and cat-calls for the baddies, and warning cries of "Watch out, 'e's be'ind yeh." And "Eh up!" for the goodies, while the pianist struggled with a suitable tempo for what was happening on the screen.

We always went home longing for the next Saturday and the next episode. Would the heroine (left tied to the track with the train puffing towards her) be rescued? Sometimes it was an Edgar Wallace thriller and we'd be left with the shadow of the Green Archer ready to strike his latest victim. This was very scary.

On the way home we'd play in the pit, a huge area with swings at one end. It was used for soap-boxing, at election time it was particularly busy. It was great to hear the hecklers and the witty replies of the politicians promising to change the world.

We couldn't go out to play on Sundays because our Sunday best was kept strictly for Church and Sunday School – or sometimes for going somewhere special, but that wasn't often. Any child who had a birthday in the week rang the bells in Sunday School.

The bells hung from a stand on the platform. When it was my turn I was given a box to stand on and a little hammer to hit the five bells. What an honour! After the sermon, the birthday children were the ones to carry round the plates, as the collection hymn was sung:

> *'Do you see this penny, it was brought by me*
> *For the little children far across the sea.*
> *Hurry penny quickly, though you are so small,*
> *Help us tell the heathen Jesus loves us all.'*

Then the other children marched around singing:

> *'Hear the pennies dropping,*
> *Listen how they fall,*
> *Every one for Jesus,*
> *He shall have them all.*
> *Dropping, dropping dropping,*
> *He shall have them all.'*

Then we were told how the children of the Dark Continent were made to bow down to idols of wood and stone. "So don't forget to bring your pennies."

Reaching five meant I could go the the Big Treat when the Sunday School children were taken on a real outing, not simply to the field which was part of Liverpool Football Club's ground – the field where the players trained. Here we ran races, played team games and were given refreshment in a paper bag – a sandwich, a scone and a cake – and afterwards marched back to the Church Hall in Walton Breck Road and dispersed from there for home.

The Big Treat was different. My birthday was too late to go with the others the year I was five, and I thought the time would never pass until the next Big Treat. But it did come, and it was to Halewood we were going.

Cherries were cheap and we saved the stones. We called them 'wags' or 'wobs' and on Treat Days going early to the Hall for a battle with the boys, we left the road covered with them, before we set off singing in the charabanc to enjoy the day.

There were a few calamities, like the two who walked on a pond covered with algae thinking it was lovely green grass. A few others had fed their tickets to the pigs and were crying because the tickets had to be handed in for refreshments. We sat at long tables in a large marquee. Eventually it was sorted out and everyone was happy. We didn't pay much for the Big Treat. A Church Bazaar at Christmas helped to fund it.

Every Wednesday, the Scripture Reader called with a case of sweets. As soon as the door was opened he'd say, "Hello, hello! Have you been good children?" to Edie and me, and we'd look at each other wondering if he'd heard us singing the parody of a hymn in Church.

While the adults talked, we kept our eyes on the case resting on his knees. What would he have in it this week? Dolly Mixtures perhaps, Licorice Allsorts or even chocolate. We were kept in suspense until the last minute but always got something.

Dad didn't think sweets were good for children. The ones we bought with our Saturday penny didn't last very long, at least mine didn't. Edie had hers long after mine had gone. She'd keep showing them to me and laughing.

But I'd be starting school soon and loved the idea of it.

Edie said, "It's soppy, school. I'm never going."

"You have to go, everyone has to go."

Mam said, "What are you arguing about, you two?"

"Doesn't everyone have to go to school, mam?"

"Yes."

"Edie says she's not going."

"She is when the time comes."

"No I'm not. I'm not always going to be readin' books."

"I want to go anyway."

"Well I'm glad you won't be here."

"So am I."

"That's enough. You're starting school on Monday, Flo."

 Chapter 2

The holidays were over and the term had begun. Children of all ages were on their way to school. And so was I. Stepping out of the door holding my mother's hand, I was dressed in a dark dress with a white starched pinafore over it, a long coat, and button boots on my feet.

Up and down our street, doors slammed and children screamed. The school I should have gone to, Venice Street Infants, had been taken over for wounded prisoners of war, though people were so hostile about them that the German prisoners had to be sent elsewhere and it was our own wounded soldiers who were now housed in the school.

Walking down the street, we met Lily and her mother. This was her first morning as well. I knew Lily by sight but she was never allowed to play out with us.

Granton Road School reminded me of a prison with its high walls and a huge clanging bell in the thick wooden door. We sang a song in time with the bell:

> *Come to school*
> *Don't be late*
> *Bring your pencil*
> *And your slate*

Lily and I were taken to the babies' class. We gave our names. "Lily Broderick", and "Florence Louise Titherington".

We sat in baby chairs with round backs. In the big grate, the fire had a guard around it.

We played with sand-trays and shells. Some of the children had to be taken home because they were crying so much. They were the 'one family' children — 'only children' as we'd call them nowadays — and there weren't many of them then.

At home, nobody asked whether I liked being at school. You just had to get on with it. No hugs, no kisses. Children had to be seen but not heard.

After school, Edie collected me. "Shall we go and see if the old ladies have put anything out?" she said.

A few doors down the street, a mother and daughter lived. Every so often, they cleared the house and put things they didn't want any longer on the back step for children to take. Edie always took the bric-a-brac while I took the books.

I love cats and when ours died and we didn't get another one, I did my best to replace it. Whenever I saw a cat I'd try to make it follow me home.

"Here she is with another cat," one of the boys would say,

chasing the poor thing away.

But I never stopped trying until one day, a big cat that I'd brought home managed to get into the meat safe in the yard and feasted on the weekend joint. I had to take the cat back to where I'd found it, but it kept following me back again. Eventually I managed to lose it and was warned never to bring another cat home.

We did get a cat though – because we had a mouse take up residence in the back kitchen. We already had a dog. The people next door had a parrot. They used to put it out on the wall next to our shed. It was always saying, "Time to get up, Harry!" A few people had parrots which they generally kept in cages hung by the front door. On their way to school, children would stand underneath saying, "Hello Polly!" This sometimes made them late for school as the huge door was locked promptly at nine o'clock.

After a morning at Granton Road School, we'd usually go home to a plate of boiled rice with sultanas in it. In the afternoon, we had our lessons in the Anfield Weslyan Church. The children who had been there in the morning went to school in the afternoon. This went on until the end of the war when the wounded soldiers were moved out and we got our Venice Street School back.

On our way to the church, we passed the football ground, where goats belonging to the cowkeeper grazed on the grassy slope at the back of the Kop.

On Duck Apple Night – or Halloween as it's called nowadays – the boys had a great time rigging up a line with apples tied to it at regular intervals. Blindfolded and with our hands behind our backs we had to try and bite an apple, though sometimes it was a piece of soap we bit on that the boys had tied on secretly and guided into our mouths. Then it was time to duck for apples bobbing about in a bowl of water.

Halloween was Edie's birthday and she always got the biggest apple father could find. Then we had to tidy up and go to bed.

Even when we were older, we had to go to bed at ten o'clock. If we were talking too much in bed, father would shout upstairs, "Pack up there." Under our breath we'd say cheekily, "We have no bag," and giggle hysterically, although we'd said it so often before.

As Lily and I were both able to read, we were moved out of the babies' class and we became firm friends, going to school and coming home together. One day on the way home, we met some of the boys. They didn't like ro be seen talking to girls, but didn't mind playing with them to make up a team.

"Playing rounders tonight?" Tommy called.

"Yes," I said. But Lily wasn't allowed to play in the street. Tommy was the only one with a bat and ball and the game finished when he was called in. We had to be careful not to offend him or he'd take the bat in. We played at the bottom of our street. One side was a brick wall and the other a long entrance to the shippen. 'Fagging' – or fielding – across the main road it was quite safe as there was very little traffic and what there was you heard coming while it was still a long way off.

On dark nights, we played guessing outside the brightly lit sweet shop windows until we were called in for bed.

"School in the morning," father would say.

"I haven't got to go," Edie protested.

"You will soon, and you need your beauty sleep."

It was no use lingering because we had to be asleep in the single bed in our parents' room by the time they came to bed. We used to do all kinds of tricks like standing on our heads to see how far we could get up the wall until we heard their footsteps on the stairs, then we'd scramble under the blankets pretending to be asleep.

There was a text hanging on the wall, '*Thou God seest me*', which was pointed out to us when we misbehaved.

One day we managed to get hold of a box of Phulnana face powder and plastered our faces with it then went to sleep, to be awakened by the horrified voice of my mother saying, "My God, what's the matter with these children?"

There was a walk-in cupboard under the stairs and we spent a lot of time in it. We used to dress up and entertain the family by acting out nursery rhymes. This one time I had a brilliant idea. I persuaded Edie to be the cow and to fill her mouth with water and spit it out as I milked her. It shocked our parents and we were sent to bed.

"I told you I didn't want to be the cow," Edie grumbled.

"Oh, shut up and go to sleep."

Queenie, our oldest sister, slept in the middle room with Dolly, the next one. When Queenie got married, Edie and I moved in with Dolly. It was terrible! The other two were fatter than me and lying between them I felt like the slice of meat in a sandwich. The bed was always lumpy, and I was always complaining.

Dolly said, "For Heaven's sake, shut up! You're like the princess who slept on a pea."

In the parlour there was an American organ and a piano which we couldn't touch. We were only allowed in the parlour when visitors came. There wasn't much room in there, what with the green plush suite and chairs to match. On the mantelpiece were two marley horses flanked by white marble figures in glass cases. A corner cupboard held some fascinating things, the best of which was the glass walking stick with a cork in the handle, filled with those brightly coloured sweets called 'hundreds and thousands'.

"I dare you to take the cork out," Edie said. "You do it," I told her. But we never did, fearing the consequences.

When a rich uncle, aunt and cousin came at night, we had to

go in the parlour. They left their fur coats on the chair and we used to try them on, taking care to put them back in the same position afterwards. "I hope they give us some money," Edie said. And they did! They gave us a whole shilling. Twelve pennies. It was like a fortune to us. We couldn't spend it all at once, we had to save some of it.

One of our daytime visitors the boys called 'Sweet Muchacha'. She wore a feather boa and when she tossed it over her shoulder and said, "Have you heard about ..." Mother would say, "Go and play in the yard. Little pitchers have big ears!" So we never heard anything, although we tried our best. Another visitor was a very tall women who wore a hat like a plant pot and a black knitted shawl and big boots. The boys called her 'Fairy Flannel Feet'. She wasn't married and kept house for a doctor.

When we had visitors for tea we had to play in the yard until they'd finished, hoping they'd leave enough for us. My father was very particular about manners. "No elbows on the table." "Sit up straight, don't lounge!"

We were not allowed to buy comics, although we read other people's, hiding them when father was in. Also, he didn't like anybody banging up against his chair when he was sitting in it. He never went to a dentist. When a tooth ached he used a penknife and, leaning on the arm of an upright chair, would eventually dig it out. Our chairs were upright too. The long bench which we sat on at mealtimes made us sit properly.

The big dresser had drawers in the front which were supposed to be for scarves and gloves but were actually stuffed with string and wool and sewing cotton which all got tangled up. When it got to the stage that the drawer would no longer shut, mam used to spread a newspaper on the floor, turn the drawer upside down on it and say, "All collect what you want and the rest will go in the bin." Then there was a scramble to pick out things we thought we needed before mother threw them out. There were always the same things that went back into the drawer time and time again.

An epidemic of diphtheria affected many of the children in our street. Edie was one of them. She was taken to hospital, then men from the Corporation came and sprayed every room in the house with disinfectant, leaving it all smelly and damp. I had to stay away from school for fear of infection.

As the only telephone available was the Undertaker's, we had to go there and ring the hospital. I can still remember my mother saying the number, "Old Swan 78". Some of the children who were taken to hospital with diphtheria never came back.

 Chapter 3

Christmas Day was the culmination of weeks of expectation for my sister Edie and me. We'd watch all the preparations and the bun-loaves being mixed and put into the big tins borrowed from the bake house in Beacon Lane. My two brothers had taken them to be baked and had brought back two tallies identical to the ones put on the bun-loaves to make sure you got the right ones back.

I tried to forget the year before, when we had found the two big bottles of dried fruit in the walk-in cupboard under the stairs that mam had been buying (when she could afford it) ready for the bun-loaves at Christmas. Edie and I had helped ourselves to them, even taking some out in pieces of newspaper pretending they were sweets. Playing in the cupboard so often aroused suspicion and we were found out. We were never tempted again because after that the bottles of dried fruit disappeared.

Christmas Eve came and the coal fire was lit under the brick boiler in the corner of the back kitchen. The big tin bath was brought in from the yard and put in front of a roaring fire. While the older ones went out carol singing, Edie and I were bathed in good carbolic soap. Then we sat by the fire in our nighties, drinking cocoa and stretching it out as long as possible until our hair dried and we were chased off to bed. We lay in bed savouring the lovely smells of roasting meat and baking cakes that drifters up from the kitchen oven, wondering if Father Christmas would bring the things we'd asked for in the notes we'd sent floating up the chimney.

Waking up at the first glimpse of light, we'd creep downstairs. "He's been!" Edie was always the first to shout as we saw the stockings hanging over the fireplace. Christmas Day had begun! Not being able to stretch over the fire guard, we had to wait patiently for someone else to come down. We'd been downstairs once already, but as it was only midnight, we were chased back to bed!

Eventually we'd get the stockings. They were father's long socks. We each had a sweet club, a smoker's kit made of chocolate, coloured chalks, a slate pencil, an orange, an apple and a bright new penny. The sweets had to be left until after dinner. When it got to the pudding we were so anxious to find the threepenny bits we hoped were in it that father would say "Take your time or you'll be sick."

"No we won't," Edie said, "It's Dolly who's sick."

"Don't be cheeky."

"Well she was sick when we went to the market."

One evening in Christmas week, dad always used to take us out for a pork pie at Harry Petty's Cocoa Rooms, and in to the market for some sweets afterwards. This year when we got home, Dolly was sick.

"That's it," said mother, "no more outings!"

"It's not fair," we protested, "we weren't sick. We can go can't we?"

But it was no good, that was it. We were disgusted with Dolly.

Only rich people had a Christmas tree, but our house was decorated with paper chains, lanterns, fans and bows we made ourselves. Everybody posted cards – after all, postage was only a penny. Just after dinner the postman came. He'd leave his cart at the end of the street as he was offered a drink at nearly every house. It was amazing he managed to finish his round! Well, it was Christmas. Most people gave him a tip too. A postman's wages weren't very good.

For the rest of the day we had a great time playing cards and board games with everybody joining in. It was a wonderful day and for once, tired and happy, we were glad to go to bed.

After Christmas, we were back into the routine of Church three times on a Sunday and school the rest of the week. Lily and I both went into the next class, still sitting together. The last lesson in the morning was arithmetic and whoever finished first was allowed to go early.

We were always first to hand our books in so we played on the swings until all the others came out too, then we joined them and went home. A strict watch was kept on the time, as there had to be a good explanation if we were even a little late.

After a few weeks we were called out by the teacher and told

"You couldn't be finished so quickly and both get the sums correct. You must be working together or one of you is copying."

She banished Lily to the back of the class. However, this didn't change anything. As soon as one of us finished and was let out, the other quickly followed. The teacher had to admit we weren't cheating, but we weren't allowed to sit together again.

A lot of school time was spent practising for concerts to give to our wounded soldiers. They wore blue uniforms to distinguish them from civilians who looked fit enough to fight, many of whom were given white feathers. There was so much patriotism then, men who were joining the army marched along the street and others joined them along the way to the cheers of the crowds.

There were popular songs about how wonderful it was in the army and posters everywhere with Lord Kitchener pointing a finger to tell us 'Your King and country needs you.' People spoke of the 'war to end all wars' and the politicians said it would be over in six months. But no one believed them. "Those who make wars should fight in them." everyone said.

Playing on the swings before the others came out at dinner time stopped when Edie started school. "I'm going to tell mam you don't go straight home." she said.

"Don't be so mean."

"Well I won't tell if you give me ..."

Whenever she wanted something of mine she always got it. She'd wait until we were having tea and if I hadn't given it to her she'd start to mutter, quietly at first and then louder and louder until mother − who was rather deaf − said "What's she saying?"

"Nothing mam," I'd say quickly. And in a whisper "You can have it Edie."

This went on all the time. She could always find something to threaten to tell mother about. As she'd been very ill, Edie mustn't ever be upset, and so she always managed to get what she wanted.

In one class I was in, we had large green text books called 'Highroads to History' which were very dull, so I took out a fairy tale book and hid it inside my history book and was so engrossed in it that when it came to my turn to read aloud, I didn't hear the teacher. She came round behind me and when she saw what I was doing she snatched the story book away.

"If you're not interested in history," she said, "you can go back to the infants' class."

This was bad enough, but Edie found out and made the most of it, so trouble at school meant trouble at home.

When we got our pennies we always spent them at our favourite sweet shop in Robson Street. Most shopkeepers had no time for children but the lady in there was very nice to us. "It's my birthday." I told her one day. She gave me a bar of chocolate and then gave Edie one. "It's not her birthday." I said.

"Oh," said the lady, "I thought you were twins."

"She's older than me." Edie said.

She was delighted with herself, but I wasn't, especially when she told the family. Mother said "You'll have to grow a bit more.

You eat enough, I don't know where you put it."

"Her arms and legs are hollow!" said Jack.

"Yes!" Alf laughed. "If she goes over a grid she'll fall in!"

"No, no! She'd be all right — her ears would catch on the bars and save her!"

"Take no notice." mother said, "Get a jar from the kitchen and go to that little shop by the Picture House and get it filled with treacle for me."

This shop was a fascinating place, so crowded with goods that you had to thread your way between barrels of treacle, syrup and paraffin. There were matches, candles, gas mantles, blocks of salt. On the way home we had a little dip out of the treacle jar, but not too much or mother would notice and send us back with it.

When Jack was seventeen he joined the army. Things were very different then. The people whose sons were still at home said they wouldn't let them volunteer, they'd wait until they were called up, and maybe the war would be over before then.

Jack was sent to France. As there wasn't radio or television, we had to wait to hear what was happening until the paper boys came running up the street in their bare feet shouting the news from the front. "Battalion wiped out!"

"Go and get a paper," mother said, "that's Jack's lot."

Father tried to comfort her. "You don't know for sure."

"But that's his regiment I know it is."

We were all worrying until late one night when there was a loud knocking on the door. Mother jumped up in fright. "It's bad news." She said. But it wasn't — it was Jack himself!

"But they said everyone in the battalion was killed," mother said, weeping with relief.

"I wasn't there," Jack told her. "I was lucky. I'd been bitten by a horse so I was in hospital."

"Oh Jack — it's a miracle!"

In our family, this tale has been told many times. It was impossible to forget it. "It was a miracle!" we always said. We were all so relieved to see him.

Once, while Jack was home on leave and our parents were out, Edie — who had taken a candle down the yard to the lavatory — suddenly started screaming.

I was alone in the back kitchen. "They're not getting me," I thought and turned the key in the back door, locking Edie out.

Jack was upstairs resting, but on hearing the screams he jumped out of bed to investigate. Seeing flames in the yard he grabbed his overcoat and dashed out. When he'd put the fire out, Jack said the back door had been locked.

"I locked it." I said.

Edie never forgot that. She lives in South Africa now. Three years ago she came home on holiday.

"Remember when you locked the door," she said, "the time I was on fire when I had an accident with the candle, remember?"

"I didn't know it was a fire. We were told to lock the door when Jack was in bed. I *was* only seven at the time."

"Well I've still got the scar," she said, showing me. "You locked me out in the yard with my hair burning."

What had happened was that some paper had caught fire and when she bent down her hair caught too. However, Jack soon put it out with his army greatcoat.

Chapter 4

Our next door neighbour was a widow who went out to work. Edie and I went in once a week to help her with her housework. She was a very stern woman. When she was widowed, she had put her twin daughters in an orphanage and whenever they came home we could hear her shouting at them. She even used the strap on them. My mother mentioned it to her one time.

"Spare the rod and spoil the child.! she said. "They have to learn to do as they are told."

"I'm glad she's not my mother." Edie said.

"So am I. And I hate housework."

"You were born for a lady that wasn't required." I was told. And it made no difference what we thought, we still had to go next door and help.

"She likes you because you're so soft," Edie chipped in.

"Well, I don't like her."

One day she took me with her to her place of work where she had her own room. She made tea for us with a cake for me as a treat.

"I'm glad it wasn't me," Edie laughed when we came back. "She can keep that shilling she gives us. I don't care."

The lady on the other side was a lot younger and she was

lovely. When we were sent on a message for her she always gave us a reward, maybe a biscuit or even a penny. When she scrubbed her step she'd do ours too if it hadn't been done already. We were glad as it saved us a job!

Not only did people scrub their front step, but they did the strip of pavement outside the house as well. We never used the front door in the daytime. The house was near the top of the street and if any of us tried to go in the front the boys would shout "Go round the back."

It was a long way through the entry, creeping past the back door of the Chinese laundry. We'd heard tales of those evil foreigners and the things they did to people, things they might do to us if they caught us. Some of the lads from school would shout "Chin Chin Chinamen." outside and then run away quickly.

Later when we went into the shop, watching nervously with one hand on the open door, ready to run if necessary, we found they were nice people. The atmosphere there was warm with steam rising high in the air from the tubs of washing and the hiss of the irons as they spat on them to check they were hot enough to do the men's starched collars.

Sometimes when we got there, we'd find our own back door locked. Jack and Alf were always playing tricks on us.

The coalman came in the street with his horse and cart shouting "Coal! Coal! One and six a bag, Coal!"

It was a long way up the entry to our house. "Catch him while he's at the bottom, before he gets too far away."

We had to run after him quick. The coalman hated having to trudge all the way back once they'd got to the top of the street.

"I want you to take this parcel to Caroline's."

"But Caroline's a witch!"

"Don't be silly — just go."

"Well she is, she is!" Edie was always the one to argue.

Caroline lived in a very small house with a younger woman we took to be her sister. Later we found out that she was, in fact, her daughter, a modest and gentle girl unlike Caroline who was nosy and interfering.

It was dusk before we arrived at her door. The oil lamp was burning, throwing shadows on the ceiling above our heads as we sat there on a form, but otherwise barely giving out any light.

"I'll get you a story Rachel used to read." Caroline said, and bringing out a bundle of papers she crouched under the flickering lamp. She must have seen the look on our faces because she said, "It's all right — it just needs sorting out. Yes, here we are ..." and she handed us a book called 'Jessica's First Prayer'. Perhaps she wasn't a witch then. Perhaps she was a Christian like us.

"We've got to go, it's getting dark."

We were glad to step out into the street again. "What do

witches do?" asked Edie.

"They cast a spell on you to turn you into a frog or a cat and you have to do anything they want you to until they take the spell off you."

"D'you know that Fatty Bates, the cookery teacher?"

"I don't like her. She told me to lie down on the floor for fire drill and when I wouldn't she chased me out to buy a hapenny carrot and an onion."

"She threw the dish-cloth at me, so I threw it back, but don't tell mam!"

"It's you that's a clat-tale."

"Only when you've got something I want."

When we got home Edie said, "She *is* a witch!"

Dolly said, "Don't be stupid."

"It's all right for you. You didn't have to go."

"What's that noise?" Jack had followed us in.

"It's only Alf doing his violin practice."

"Sounds like a pig in pain!"

"Just because you're not musical."

"You two come and get your teas. There aren't any witches."

I knew about witches. I'd read all about them in my books and once you'd got a spell on you only the Good Fairy could take it away. That's why I was frightened to go to bed without a candle. Edie was scared too, that's why she took a candle down the yard and got burnt.

On saturday we had to go to the dairy for the milk for Sunday's rice pudding. Mrs Hargreaves the cowkeeper was a big un-smiling woman. She was scrupulously clean and her dairy always looked as though it had just been scrubbed. She had two sons with shiny faces who always looked as though they'd just been scrubbed too! She was very strict with them and never allowed them into the dairy.

The huge brown pan-mug was yellow inside with a ladle hanging on it, and on a shelf a black and white china cow stared into space.

"Take your lid off."

We meekly did as we were told and handed Mrs Hargreaves our can. She took down the ladle and, dipping it into the milk, poured the exact amount into the can. "That'll be tuppence," she said, handing it to me. "And shut the door as you go out."

Walked home carefully, afraid of spilling the milk can and avoiding the shippen where the cows lived.

During a meal, nothing had to be left on the plate. If ever you did leave anything, it appeared on your plate again before the next meal.

"Never eat in the street" we were told, although we were allowed to take a piece of currant pie out and eat it from a sheet of newspaper in the back entry. We'd pick the currants out one by one and make them last.

Newspaper came in handy. Most things you bought were

wrapped in it. In the rain it often disintegrated, scattering the groceries on the pavement. Edie and I had the job of cutting sheets of newspaper into squares to hang in the lavatory threaded on a piece of string. It wasn't easy as the cat thought it was a game and was always determined to get the string for herself!

January brings the snow
Makes our feet and fingers glow

It always seemed to snow in January, and sometimes even at Christmas. It was good fun, making slides and snowmen in the street and the schoolyard, having snowball battles with the lads, watching the skaters in Stanley Park, going home ro a roaring fire and perhaps roasting chestnuts.

"My wellies are too tight," I moaned. "My feet hurt."

"There's always something hurting you. You'll get new boots when we can afford them."

Wellington boots were always black.

"Sit down and help with the rug. Cut up the rags for me."

Anything that had outgrown its usefulness was made into rag rugs with a piece of coarse sacking and a peg.

"I wanted to finish my library book."

"Yes, and be too scared to go to bed," Dolly said.

It was always a good excuse to go to the library on the way home from school. Librarians were suspicious of children and kept their eagle eyes on us. If anyone dared to whisper they'd point to the big SILENCE notice and we'd creep out with a book. What I loved were the mysteries and the wicked people in them.

> *February brings the rain*
> *thaws the frozen lake again*

Rain. Splashing through it, looking for the deep puddles where water had poured down from the gutters. If we were in trouble when we got home, well, what of it — we had fun!

"Are you having pancakes on Tuesday?"

"Yes, I love them, don't you?"

"What d'ye have on them?"

"Lemon juice of course!"

Some boys went past singing:

> *'Pancake Tuesday's a very happy day*
> *If ye don't give us a holiday*
> *We'll all run away*
> *We shall go*
> *Down Cherry Lane*
> *Here comes the teacher with a big fat cane'*

After all the rain and the bad weather we knew it was spring because the younger ones in the family had to line up for doses of brimstone and treacle.

"It's horrible!" We all said

"It'll do you good."

"Are you going out on Easter Monday?" Lily said one day.

"If it's fine we might go to Bowring Park, if they feel like taking us."

"It's at the tram terminus, isn't it? I'll be going in my uncle's three wheeled Morgan car to see my cousin Doris."

"Is she still at that Home? She was all right when she visited you that day."

"My auntie caught her trying to throw a glass bowl at her when she turned her back."

"That's terrible." Lily was the only one in her family who went to visit Doris.

In the summer, most of the holidays were spent in Stanley Park. It was a wonderful place with a boating lake, tennis courts, bowling greens, large shelter-houses — one big enough to play team games in when it rained. There were lovely walks with bowers to sit and read in, and birds in cages, and a beautiful rose garden with a floral clock underneath a plaque which said:

> *'The kiss of the sun for pardon,*
> *The song of the birds for mirth,*
> *You are nearer to God in a garden,*
> *Than anywhere else on the earth.'*

Later on, swimming baths were built in Stanley Park. On the ladies' side there were so many spectators (mostly old men) that there was a rumour going around that some of them had nearly strangled themselves trying to look through the fence, but I don't think it was true.

There was a notice on the grass verges saying *Please Keep Off The Grass* but that didn't apply to the playing fields which were fenced off from the walks. The Palm House was lovely, warm and quiet. We often ate our sandwiches there, especially if it was raining. Behind it was a balcony where a brass band played most nights of the week to a very appreciative audience.

There were always policemen in the park. Some actually lived there in houses near one or other of the two entrances. The gates were closed at one hour after sunset precisely.

In the holidays we spent a great deal of time at Stanley Park. Schools used it for rounders matches and it was always full of people.

Back at school after the holidays, we were told that the soldiers had enjoyed our concerts so much they wanted us to go and entertain their injured comrades who were unable to go out. The men were housed in our school which was being used as a hospital. Now we could visit it for the first time.

"There's a swimming pool in the cellar," one of the girls said.

"Is that right, Miss?"

"Yes, but it's not used now, It's full of coal for the fires. The place has to be kept warm."

Venice Street School is built in a square surrounded on all sides by streets of terraced houses. It has two school yards or play-grounds, one for Girls & Mixed Infants, the other for Boys.

"Come along children, don't dawdle," the teacher said, hurrying us into the hall on the day of the concert.

"It's nicer than Granton Road," the children all agreed. "But we have to go there for a few more years."

Of course the soldiers were all delighted. I suppose the songs and recitations and all reminded them of their own homes and families. Not that we were all that good mind!

"The Americans are coming here," one boy said. He always liked to think he knew everything.

"How d'ye know?"

"My brother's a copper an' he said. The Americans are coming here on their way to the war."

"I 'eard that too. They're going to Knotty Ash in the huts they've built there.

"Perhaps we'll see 'em."

"No, we'll be in school. I bet they'll come when we're in school."

"Where's America?" I asked when I got home.

"It's on the other side of the world. It used to belong to us. Explorers found it and put the British flag there. But they're on their own now."

"But why are they coming all that way to fight the Germans?"

"You ask too many questions, girl. Go out and play."

This was always the reply I got. "Don't ask too many questions. You'll know soon enough."

Chapter 5

"So, the Americans *are* coming," father said. "And about time too. We're losing so many men."

"Let's hope it finishes the war and our Jack comes home safely," mother said. "And before you have to go too, Alf."

Alf was sixteen and very different from his brother. He played the violin and sang in the Philharmonic Choir. His eyesight was very poor. Jack had good eyesight but, like Edie, no time for music and culture. Those two were very friendly while Alf and I sung together. He taught me all the baritone songs he knew.

"The Yanks are coming!" Dolly burst in. "Are you coming to see them?"

Crowds were hurrying down the streets to the main road. "They've landed at the docks and they're comin'."

"How d'ye know?"

There was always someone who knew secrets. "They weren't s'posed to be comin' till next week."

"Well they're coming now. There they are, at the top of the hill."

As they came along Walton Breck Road people ran out from all the streets. The soldiers stopped on the huge space in front of Liverpool Football Ground. They dropped their kit and everyone crowded round them as they gratefully drank the buttermilk the women had brought them. When they were ready to move on, the boys all clamoured to carry their kitbags and rifles. The girls ran alongside holding hands with the men for as far as they were allowed to go.

They gave us coins, quarters and cents, which were exchanged at the pawnbrokers for English money.

Next time the cry went up, "The Yanks are coming again!", we were in school. The headmistress came into the class with a handful of small Union Jacks. She gave them out and said, "The American soldiers are coming this way. I want you all to go out and stand on the pavement and wave your flags and cheer them along to show them how much we appreciate them coming."

"When are they coming again, Miss?"

"I don't know, but this is your turn. Another class will do it next time."

Back in school, the teacher said, "Now children, I want you to write down a description of what you have just seen." When it was time to go home, Lily was waiting for me. "Are you going to that concert tonight?"

"Yes, what are you doing?"

"My mother's ill in bed. Dolly's looking after us."

"I'll be glad when we're in our own school."

"The soldiers will all be gone then, no more concerts."

"You'll be all right doing the Sunday School ones. I don't like singing."

"Did you see all that brown stuff on the pavement outside the houses?"

"Me dad said it's because someone is very ill and can't be disturbed by people going past. It's to deaden the noise."

"Must be someone important then."

"Anyway, see you tomorrow."

"Tara!"

When I got in, Edie was there and Alf followed soon after. "You kids want to go on the lake in the park?"

"Yes, yes! Are we going now?"

"If you hurry up with your tea."

We loved going on the lake, round the island in the middle and under the fancy bridges. With Alf sweating at the oars, the wash as we passed would send the ducks and swans into a tizzy and they'd swim away indignantly swishing their tails.

There were always crowds of people in the park, especially on a summer day. Then after Church whole families strolled around the paths, watching the boats from the bridges. No games were allowed on Sundays. We couldn't even play in the street. Knitting and other handiwork had to be put away until Monday.

Sunday was observed by everyone except for one little corner shop where, if people had unexpected visitors, it was OK to knock on a side door for a tin of salmon or ham.

Sunday night Church was in the Mission Hall belonging to the

Big Church. Although we had the same order of service, the same prayers and responses, the hymns were always jollier at the Mission and we had solos from members of the congregation instead of the choir. One old man used to stagger up to the front every week and sing the same hymn:

> *'Herlas, and did my Savure bleed*
> *And did my Soverain die*
> *Did thorns surround 'is sacred 'ead*
> *For such a worm as I?'*

Boys at the back sniggered, but the sidesman behind, being there especially to keep them in order, flicked each one on the ear with his fingers.

"Wah, that hurt!" one of them whispered. It shut them up for the rest of the service!

The folk who went to the Big Church used to think they were superior to those 'mission people' as they called us, but they used the Sunday School as well as we did.

In 1916, mother had another baby. He was born on Trafalgar Day and they called him Albert Nelson. Home from school that day, father took us up to the bedroom. "This is your new brother." he said.

"Isn't he little," I said.

"Big enough for me," said mother.

"Can we go out and play now?" Edie had turned away. She wasn't the baby any longer. It was nothing new to us, just one of those things. Everyone had babies. We asked no questions – we couldn't think of any.

All kinds of people came to see the baby. Caroline was there when we went upstairs. She was sitting between my father and Queenie who was staying while mother was in bed. Caroline emphasised her points by patting the knee next to her own with a heavy hand. Queenie got fed up with this and sid, "I'll have to sit on the other side. This knee's bruised."

Caroline never took offence. She loved coming to our house. She'd always say she'd only come for a minute but then she'd stay and stay until father had to start his yawing ploy. He'd start it off and soon everyone was yawning!

"Oh, I'll have to be going, Mr Titherin," she'd say, falling for it every time.

Baby Albert was very delicate and needed a lot of attention which gave us more freedom. On the way home from school, Edie met me and said, "Let's go the swings in the pit."

"I'll come with you then."

"All right, but don't you tell. We can get in through the bandy railings."

When we got home mother said, "You're late. Where have you been, you two?"

"Dolly said, "They've been to the pit, I saw them."

We went outside. Dolly followed us. "You know you've to come straight home."

We both chanted together,

'Clat tale tit
your tongue shall be slit
and all the dogs in Liverpool
Shall have a little bit.'

"Well, I had to go to Johnson's and you too were supposed to go too."

We laughed and said, "Well, I'm glad we didn't." together.

"You two are like parrots," Dolly said, "always saying everything together."

Sometimes we were very pally, Edie and me. When Violet, a friend of Edie's, called for her we'd go into the street to play. If the boys were playing leap frog I'd join in.

Sometimes we played 'Ten Ton Weight' when the biggest boy would put his hands on the wall and the others jumped one by one onto his back with legs astride, like riding a horse. I'd just had my turn once when Alf came up the street and called me over. "Girls shouldn't be playing that sort of game," he said and took me indoors. But he didn't say anything to mother about it, he just said, "Have you got a book to read?"

Chapter 6

"They say the war will be over soon, now the Yanks are in it."

"Who are they?"

"You know, the politicians."

We were standing with a crowd of people watching the monkey man who was sitting in his shop window mending boots. He had a small monkey on his shoulder. It was dressed in a red jacket and a red fez. The monkey put his arms round the man's neck. He gave it a nut. On its long chain it jumped down and sat eating the nut. The man went on with his work.

"It's a good job the animal has a hat on or you wouldn't know which was which!"

"Aye you're right there. He's a good cobbler though, I'll give you that. The men moved away.

Edie pulled on my arm. "Come on Florrie. You'd stay here all day, wouldn't you?"

"Where have you been?" Dolly said when we got home. "Mam's been looking for you."

"Watching the monkey."

"They're saying the war will soon be over."

"Who are saying?"

"Some men in the crowd."

"There's a concert for the soldiers tonight in the Church. All our class are in it. The boys in uniform, the girls as nurses."

"I'm singing by myself," I told them, "with a big red cross on the front of my uniform."

"You'll look daft." Edie said.

"Just because you're at the back ..."

"Stop your arguing, you two."

The concert was a huge success. My song, 'The Rose that Grows in No-Man's Land' received an ovation. I was thrilled and boasted about it at home.

"Self praise is not good for you."

"I knew I could do it."

"You're too confident."

It was years later when I heard all about Edith Cavell that I realised it was the song they were applauding so passionately. Not the singer but the song. Some of the soldiers in the audience had been rescued by her themselves.

Now some of the Americans began to come back wounded. We were allowed to go and see them in the make-shift hospital. Two in particular were my favourites — Ben and Joe. They were both black. Joe had lost and arm and Ben had lost both legs. When it was fine they sat in wheelchairs in the school yard. They were always very cheerful in spite of their injuries and made me laugh with their stories about life 'back home' in America. I went home very puzzled – surely all black people live in Africa.

"No," said father, "you'll learn about it later."

"Yeh never get to know anything here."

"What did you say?"

"Nothing dad!"

In the meantime, we were proceeding with our schooling. Some of the teachers had been called up for military service and been replaced by others who had come out of retirement. Sometimes we had students who were still at college but released for a term or two to help out.

A French woman who took Dolly's class called out, "Tingtong Doris," as she took the register. From then on, that was the nickname that Dolly had.

Another teacher was Mr Luny. He was a small, bad–tempered man with a white beard. He took a dislike to one particular girl and made her stand behind the blackboard for the least thing. Once, when he caught her peeping out from behind the blackboard to make everyone laugh, he dragged her out and hit her. She dashed out of the room shouting, "Luny by name and loony by nature."

She was an only child and the next day her mother came to school to complain. "People like you shouldn't be teaching girls." she said, "I'll make sure this doesn't happen again."

"The school doctor's coming tomorrow." we were told, "and the nurse." We all groaned. That meant that we'd have to have a bath, even though it wasn't Saturday. Mother would have to go through our hair with a small-toothed comb looking for nits. Of course, some families didn't bother, but we all knew they were dirty and had flea bites.

The doctor tested our eyes and ears and sounded chests. The nurse used two sticks to look through our hair. Edie was upset when we got home. "They want to see you," she told mother.

It turned out her eyesight as very poor and she'd have to wear glasses. No wonder she didn't read − she hadn't been able to see the page in front of her!

As most people couldn't afford to buy them, the glasses Edie got were steel-rimmed, terrible things supplied by the Education Authority.

We never had toothbrushes and never went to the dentist. People like us couldn't afford such things. If you got toothache, father tied a piece of cotton around the tooth with the other end round the door knob. He'd bang the door shut and the tooth would come out on the end of the cotton. Stomach-ache was cured with Glauber Salts. You went to school with whatever ailment you had, unless it was infectious.

One morning when mother was still in bed I showed Dolly that I had a rash all over me. "You'd better wait until mam comes down." she said. She came down at five-to-nine by which time the rash had gone. I had to run to school, which brought it back again. A visit to the clinic didn't help at all, and even the doctor didn't know what it was.

In winter, when the weather was cold, the oven shelf was wrapped in a towel and put in our bed. It caused a bit of trouble between the three of us as it soon grew cold.

As we grew older, the cosy Saturday nights having a bath in front of the fire stopped. Now we bathed on Mondays after the washing had been done, while the back boiler was still lit. The tin bath was brought into the kitchen and afterwards, the soapy water was swilled down the yard.

As we set off for school one morning, Edie asked, "Is that boy calling for you?"

"Yes, why?"

"I don't like him."

"Well, I do!"

He lived in Louisa Street, the next one above ours. He had to pass our door. He gave me a glass bangle. Edie took it and put it on. She flexed her arm muscles and the bangle broke. She handed me the pieces saying, "It was no good anyway."

"Don't forget you have to call for Mary," Dolly said. Mary lived in the next street and was always late. The teacher had told us to call for her. I was on pins waiting, she was never ready and we'd all be late.

When we played skipping together, the boys joined in too sometimes. "They always turn the rope too fast, the boys."

"That's 'cos you're too fat."

"I'm not fat. They don't call me skinamalinks like you!"

Everybody had to take a turn with the rope. We sang skipping rhymes as we turned it:

'All in together girls,
This fine weather girls ..."

or

"I saw Peter sitting on a chimney pot ..."

And shouting, though we didn't know what a Zeppelin was:

'A Zeppelin, a Zeppelin, a bomb!"

"Are you going to Doris' concert?

Doris had a big bottle of water and a packet of lemonade powder. She kept filling the bottle from somewhere although she couldn't have got into the house, the door was locked. Afterwards I found out that she had been dipping the bottle into the lavatory and making the lemonade with that!

The street was crowded with people overflowing onto the main road. Paper boys were shouting, "Special Edition — Echo or Express — Special Edition!"

"Flora!" mother called (she called me that sometimes), "Take a penny off the dresser and run out for a paper."

That day the atmosphere was very different from what it had been three years before. People were cheering now and throwing their arms round one another.

"It's over," they were saying. "The war's over, they've declared an Armistice and the Germans have surrendered."

"Now we'll get our school back," Edie said, "It's nearer than that rotten Granton Road."

"Will the Americans go home now?"

"Of course they will, stupid."

"Now Edie, there's no need for that."

"But mam, she's always talking about the Yanks."

"Oh come on, let's go out to play."

"No, I don't like crowds."

"Yeh too scared!"

The Americans had started packing to go home. "I'll never forget you," said Sam.

"And I won't either," said Ben. "But we'll not be going until after Christmas. Before we say goodbye, we're going to lay on a party for you all".

And they did – and it was lovely. They produced all the things we'd never had because of the war; balloons, crackers, fancy hats, fairy lights, cream cakes and lemonade – the real stuff made with fresh lemons not powder.

When they did go, it left a big gap in our lives. The fighting was over but a different war was just beginning – the fight against poverty and deprivation. Even shopkeepers found it hard to manage. The notice in the corner ship read

'Please do not ask for credit'
as a refusal often offends.'

"Run to the shop for half a pound of cheese," mother would say, "and if you fall, don't stop to pick yourself up."

In the shop Edie said, "Look, what does that notice say?"

"The clock's got no fingers," I read, "No tick here! Why don't you wear your glasses?"

"They're awful. You wouldn't wear them. You're lucky."

"I know I am."

When Jack came home it was joy mixed with sadness, for Queenie's husband had been killed a few months before and she'd taken the baby to Kent to her husband's parents.

Eventually when the Yanks had gone for good we moved back into our own school. There was new headmaster called Tetley. The boys made up a rhyme:

'Mr Tetley's a very good man
Goes to Church on Sunday
Prays to God to give him strength
To cane the boys on Monday.'

Chapter 7

There wasn't much work anywhere now. When people met, it was a regular thing to say, "Are you working?"

"No, are you?"

They even made a song about it.

Father worked at the docks. He was a Quay Foreman and it was up to him to choose the men each day who would work alongside him. Father wasn't comfortable about this. He didn't like turning men away. He didn't like to think of the children waiting at the dock gates hoping their dads had been lucky this time and been selected to work. He didn't like to think of the unlucky ones who would have nothing to take home.

There were children stopping the men on their way home from work asking, "Any bread left?" They were terrible times.

They'd been through hard times themselves, our parents. When they were first married, before any of us were born, they'd been starving and so desperate that father had thought of joining the army in Ireland, the Black and Tans. Mother talked him out of that idea. Mother knew about poverty too. When a friend came with a hard-luck story, she'd always try to help if she could.

When things were at their worst, some children were actually sewn into their clothes, partly to keep them warm, but mainly because they had no other clothes, nothing for them to change into, so they kept the clothes on day and night till the spring came. Our family was lucky. Jack found a job at the Ministry of Pensions and Alf was in a Brewer's Office.

Living as we did between two famous football grounds, the weekends were spent discussing the relative merits of the Liverpool and Everton teams. Our household — like many others in that district — were fiercely divided about this, which gave us plenty to argue about.

The matches were played on Wednesdays, which meant there were always taxis flying around the streets. A girl from our school had been run down by one and lost a leg. To avoid accidents of that sort, we were allowed to go home early when there was a match on. But of course we didn't go home, did we! We went to the steps of the football ground, to the Kop where the gates were opened at three-quarter time and we could watch the game for nothing.

"Make way for the shareholders" the spectators would shout, moving aside a little so that we could see the players. Before long, the school heard what we were up to and banned us from going, but we still sneaked along to the Kop, hoping no one would tell on us.

The football crowd were a law-abiding lot. There was no

singing, no trouble, no enmity between supporters, just friendly rivalry and jokey comments.

Liverpool had a goal-keeper who swore a lot. And a preacher tried to reform him. 'Derby Games' are what they call matches between two teams from the same town. In our case, Everton v Liverpool — and these were always extra exciting.

Before I was old enough to go to a match with my brothers, we could hear the roar of the crowd when a goal was scored from home. I'd often be sent out when the game was finished to find out who'd won. "It was Everton."

"Are you sure? Did you ask anybody?"

"There was no need. It was obvious!" All the Everton lot in their blue scarves were talking while those supporters with red scarves were looking pretty glum.

The matches were played on Saturdays then, and we still went down the hills to the market on that day. Everything was cheaper there. Eggs were 11p a dozen. We seemed to be buying more and more every week. The bags seemed to get heavier all the time. Still, the afternoon matinee at the Picture House made up for it.

On Sundays, as we weren't allowed to play in the street, we played quietly in our yard. We'd make a tent from coats and stools and sit in it until it was time for Sunday School. Then we'd come home again for tea.

Mother baked pies for Sunday, apple and currant on large plates. We were given one slice of each and we sat round the table singing hymns until the bells called us to church.

In school on Monday, we took a penny for the bank with a card that said;

'Take care of the pennies and the pounds will take care of themselves.'

The English teacher was very fond of grammar. After dictation, the work had to be read out loud. One girl had written, "I laid the table."

Miss said, "Hens lay eggs. You do not lay tables."

Most of the teachers had nick-names, children spotting any quirk or handicap. A master who resembled a comedian of the day was called Ambrose. We always knew what he'd had for breakfast by his tie.

Mr Smith was a dashing debonair type dedicated to teaching, he spent a lot of time after school with the football tram. Unlike the others, he never complained about our shoes not being polished. He knew how it was for poor families, the constant struggle to keep the children clean and tidy.

The next headmaster was very fond of music. His lessons were never dull. Anybody caught talking was 'neighbourin', neighbourin'. He always said everything twice. Should anyone glance towards the window during his lessons he'd say they were 'rubber neckin'.

He was slightly deaf and would always ask, "What, what?". So he was known as Daddy Wat. He trained the choir for massed singing in Picton Hall or St George's Hall. If the weather was too bad for games the boys had to join the singing class.

Daddy Wat had a unique way of choosing his choir. He'd go round the class stopping to listen to us one by one with his ear to each mouth. To the girls he'd say, "Sing up, sing up!" and to the boys or the poor singers he'd say, "Out, go out grunter!" To those kids who simply couldn't sing he'd say, "Get a book and read", which is something we still say today if someone's trying to sing but is making an awful noise.

The teachers were always well dressed, the men in dark suits, the women in plain dark dresses or tweed costumes and mostly white blouses, neat and modest. The only one who was different was a young woman teacher who wore plunging necklines by those standards. It caused a bit of a stir among children and parents. Such things simple weren't done!

The school prize giving was held, not in the evening with proud parents looking on, as happens today, but in school time at an ordinary school assembly. I received a large brass medal once with the inscription:

'For good conduct and regular attendance over three years.'

Later, I received another one, a gilt one this time, for four years' good conduct. I still have it.

There was a man called Major Lester who organised free

dinners for those boys who came from very poor homes. In some cases, their fathers had not returned from the war, in others, the man had returned but crippled or blinded or suffering from being gassed in the trenches and unable to work. For the very poor, the police supplied trousers and clogs.

The only work a woman could get was domestic, daily charring for a middle class family perhaps. Or, if she was single, she'd go into service at a big house.

Thinking how things are today in the 1990s, it seems strange to think of the rivalry there was between children then for any job that was available, such as delivering milk for the cow-keeper, fruit and vegetables for the grocer, or newspapers morning and evening.

In one of our shops a notice read

'Man is dust. Dust settles. Be a man.'

I had to have that explained to me. Father said, "It means that any debts should be settled quickly. If you'd had goods on credit, say."

"Goods on credit!" I said, astonished. I knew no one allowed that.

"Not these days," said father. "Before the war, it was common practice, but not in these difficult times."

Chapter 8

Trying to keep some of the people occupied, the Liverpool Corporation decided to have a Civic Week and open the principal buildings in the town to the public. Schools had to take the children as they weren't allowed to go by themselves.

When going out anywhere with the school, we were told well in advance to ensure that everyone was presentable with gym-slips pressed, blouses snowy white and boots polished to such a shine "You could see your face in them" as teacher said.

Some of the boys used Zebo grate polish. Mixed with water, a small slab of it was enough for a whole grate and, for those not able to afford Cherry Blossom, some over for the boots. Zebo protected the leather and polished up a treat.

When the teacher was satisfied with our appearance and had made sure we each had a penny for the fare, we set out in an orderly crocodile for the tram that would take us to the Liver Building. It was very exciting going up in the lift to the Liver Clock. When the lift stopped, we stepped out onto a platform.

"Children, come and look at the view."

From Garston to Seaforth the docks were full of ships. They had funnels of every colour and from where we were stars and stripes merged into one. What looked like a toy train seemed to crawl along the overhead railway, which to us, was way below.

Then up the steps to the clock itself.

"Oh, it's got no hands, no fingers."

"Not like and ordinary clock, Miss, is it?"

"This clock doesn't have fingers, it just strikes the hours."

We scribbled our initials on the white-washed walls before scrambling back down to ground level again and the long walk home.

Some of the great cruisers were in the dock that week — the Canadian pacific, The Baltic, The White Star and The Montcalm. With them were two Cunarders — The Samaria and The Montrose. The public were allowed to go aboard and look around these ships as part of the Civic Week celebrations.

As the years went by, in one Civic Week after another, we managed to see over most of these great ships. Another feature of the Civic Week was an illuminated tram which went all round the city at night.

During the holidays, we'd sometimes go to New Brighton on the ferry, which was always crowded. When we got there, so was the promenade. The sands were full of children and women keeping an eye on them in deckchairs. Mother would take one for an hour while we paddled and turned the stones over to look for crabs in the pools left behind by the tide.

When her hour was up in the deckchair, mother used to retire from the beach and find a place to sit on the steps of a large building, from where she could watch us playing and the ships sailing past. Sometimes there'd be a cruiser anchored there waiting for the tide to come in and enable it to sail clear of the river and out to sea.

One day, Dolly walked into some sinking sand and was nearly sucked under but someone nearby dragged her out to safety. Her clothes were all wet and muddy and had to be dried in the breeze while she huddled under a coat shivering.

Once, on the way home, a small boy upset a bucket of crabs on the tram. It caused a riot with people jumping up to get out of the way, and the boy yelling.

Soon after this, mother bought a bell tent and we didn't go to New Brighton any more. "Just so the children can have a holiday." she told dad. We camped in a field near the shore at Leasowe and spent hours on the beach digging for cockles which were plentiful then.

Next term back at school, the headmaster made an announcement one morning in assemble after prayers. "It has been decided that this school should have a uniform. It will be a hat and blazer with the monogram V.S. on the badge."

We were thrilled. "You can have a hat but not a blazer." We couldn't afford both at once." Dolly got a blazer and it would probably be passed down to me when she grew out of it.

Lorraine Street School had hats as well with L.S. embroidered on the badges. When we played them at rounders, we called them the Lemon Suckers. They called us the Venetian Stealers.

"Have you learned the hymn about drink yet?" mother asked me. We were preparing for the Church concert.

"Yes" It goes:

> *'For the honour of dear old England,*
> *Fight the drink.*
> *For the sake of the little children,*
> *Fight the drink.*
> *Oh the victims we can save*
> *From a drunkard's early grave*
> *Let us with the good and brave*
> *Fight the drink.'*

"There's a poem as well called The Teetotal Doll. Someone always says The Drunken Doll first."

All the churches and missions preached against drink, always asking members of the congregation to go to the front and sign the pledge. The Salvation Army was particularly keen on this.

Plenty of other songs taught us the evils of drink. Even in day school we were told about it as well. When the Church started a Girl Guide company I joined and heard even more about drink there!

The Girl Guides met on Thursdays, and on Tuesdays it was th Band of Hope meeting with the same theme.

The best lesson at school was swimming. Once a week, we had to meet outside the Public Baths early in the morning. While we waited for it to open we began undressing, taking off as many clothes as we could to save time once we got inside. We only had fifteen minutes in the water training for certificates, so the faster we could get into the pool the better.

Children going to the Baths on their own rather than with the school, were supervised by fearsome women who carried long poles. Anyone trying to hide from the supervisor and stay in over the allotted time would be fished out by her with the pole which she'd hook onto their costume and drag the child to the edge and out of the water.

It was salt water in the pool, with a fresh water shower which you had to go through first, which many families used to save paying for a bath in the public bath house.

Alone in the house one day, Edie and I were reaching up to a top shelf and brought a book down. "Is that the one you wanted?" she asked.

I opened the book. "Oh look at this!" We both stared at the picture of a monkey with a little one in its stomach. "What does it say? Read it out."

"It says babies come the same way as this, we came the same

way as this baby monkey."

"I don't believe it. What's it called, the book?"

"The Origin of Species. It's written by Charles Darwin."

"Quick! Put it back, somebody's coming."

We had been told not to touch the books on the top shelf. "What are you two up to now?" mother said, coming in with Caroline. "You can go out and play, you two."

"I've got a headache," Edie said, "I don't want to go out."

"Go on with you, you can come back in if you really don't feel well."

"I feel sick, I do, I do. I feel really poorly, mam."

Later when we got back indoors, Caroline had gone. Edie was looking miserable. "It's measles," said mother, "she has a rash. We'll have to go to the clinic."

It *was* measles. Again the men came from the council and sprayed the house with disinfectant. Edie's sight being weak already, the curtains were drawn by day and the gas was kept low at night.

Mother had been trying for ages to exchange our house for a larger one, without success. We were still sleeping three in a bed. As we got older and bigger the problem as getting worse.

One day after a needlework lesson I dashed home to tell mother, "The teacher says I am the best darner in the class."

"Don't boast, Florrie." A few weeks later mother threw a huge bundle of men's socks at me. "Get busy on those girl, if you're so good at darning."

And that was my job for evermore – darning all the socks and stockings in the house. It taught me never to boast!

I took the papers home from school for a Scholarship to Skerries Typing College. Father signed them. But when I went to do the entrance exam I made a hash of it by not reading the questions carefully. It said,

'write on ONE of these subjects.'

I wrote on all three. In spite of this stupid mistake, they still offered me a place but on the condition that we paid six guineas, half the fee. Perhaps if I'd been the oldest, or indeed the youngest, it might have been different. "I'm afraid you'll have to stay where you are," dad said sadly. "We can't afford that sort of money, lass."

So that was it.

The next disappointment was the exhibition at Wembley. One girl out of each class would be sent there. She was chosen by voting. After a time it it was between me and a girl named Eileen and the voting was down to five. I was the favourite with three friends, and Eileen with two.

When it came to the final vote however, Eileen won. One of my friends had switched sides and voted for her!

"Why did she do that?" I asked one of the others.

"Oh, Eileen had been taking her to her grandmother's sweet shop every day after school."

The teacher said, "I'm sorry Florence. I'd have liked it to be you that went to London."

This cheered me up a bit, especially as I'd thought she wasn't keen on me. After all, I'd let my pencil tin drop in the middle of a lesson and it had gone skittering down the classroom steps. The tin was advertising Red Seal Toffees which were very popular.

"The next tine that is dropped, I'll forbid them in school," the teacher said.

It's seventy years ago now and I still feel bad about it. And about my so-called friend.

Mother was playing the piano when I got home, some of her Scottish Songs. "Well, that's a shame," she said when I told her about the election. "But never mind, love. Come and sing this one with me."

I knew the song. Mother had taught me it with her Scottish accent:

'When ye gang awa Jimmy
Far across the sea laddie
When ye gang to Eetaly
What will ye send me laddie?

I'll send ye a braw new goon Jinny
I'll send ye a braw new goon lassie
An' it shall be of silk and gold
With valenciens set round Jinny

When ye come back again Jimmy
From far across the sea laddie
When ye gang from Eetaly
What will ye bring me Jimmy?

When I come back again Jinny
From far across the sea lassie
I'll bring with me a gallant gay
To be your ain guid man lassie

Be my guid man yoursel' Jimmy
An tak me o'er Eetaly
With ye at home to dwell Jimmy

I dinna see how that can be Jinny
For I've a wife and bairnies three
And I'm no sure wud they agree lassie

Gey back to your wife and home jimmy
And I will pray thee ne'er may have
a broken heart like mine laddie

Dry up that tearful ee Jinny
For I've neither wide nor bairnies three
An' I'll wed none but thee lassie'

I felt better after the song as mother knew I would. "Richie's been here wanting you to go to his party."

It was great going there. Richie only had one sister who was much older than he was. We often went round together, the two of us. When we met any of his friends he'd say, "This is my cousin".

I had another 'cousin' in Tommy, who lived further down the street. I'd met him soon after they moved in. He was sitting on the wall in front of the house.

"What ya doing her," I said. "Ye don't live here."

"Yes, I do – we've just moved in."

They were very different, these two, Richie was very quiet, whereas Tommy was a comedian and very fond of music. He used to pretend to play the banjo saying, "Plinka-plonk-a-pink-a-ponk. Bubblr-alley-bum-bum."

He was very popular in our house. Even Edie liked him! In the middle of something else, he'd jump up and say, "I've got to go home to Chokin' Fanny."

"Who's that, Tommy?"

"It's me mam. When I tell her a joke at the tea table she starts to laugh and then she chokes."

When we played in his back yard, his mother provided drinks for us. We were usually rehearsing for Tommy's latest play. He was a born director. I hope he was able to get into stage work somewhere. I haven't heard anything of him in 60 years.

"Who's that crowd? He asked me one day, pointing to the photograph at the end of the lobby.

"They're all my father's family."

"I thought it was a charabanc do. Never seen so many people in one family. Do they all visit?"

"I've only met two of them. Two jolly fat aunts. I was only little. This one, I sat on her knee and when she laughed, I rolled off."

"What about all the others?"

"Never seen any of them."

It was strange to think of it – this huge family and we'd never met any of them.

There were a lot of stories going around about the Mormons at this time. You had to be careful or they'd kidnap you and ship you off to America. Then they'd force you to become someone's second wife. They all had more than one wife, it was said. Now they were running short of women and were snatching girls like us to send back home.

What with the Mormons and films about the white slave trade, we were all jolly careful if we were out after dark, thought they always told us we'd be all right, being such good little Christians.

After the others had gone to bed I'd turn the gas-light on and scare myself silly reading about Count Dracula and the tales of Dr Fumanchu and Moriarty.

"Why d'ye read them?" Alf asked.

"I love them, they're so exciting."

"There's going to be trouble." father was saying as I went in one night. "Things are getting worse."

"I agree with you Jack," my uncle said. "The Government will have to do a lot better than they're doing now. People are dying of malnutrition. It's terrible."

It was true. The poor were becoming even poorer, though many of them were too proud and did their best to hide their difficulties, not wanting others to know. When the dole ran out, people had to ask the Government for help. Then the inspectors would come to the house to see what the family could sell.

"You can sell that," they'd say. "You can sell the piano."

For many families, there was nothing left that could be sold. And anyway, there was no one with the money to buy. Even a man's suit, the one thing he had left, was pawned on Monday, his poor wife slipping in at the side door of the pawn shop to avoid the shame of it.

The pittance raised would often be spent on drink, the only way to escape their troubles. If he was lucky, the man's suit would be redeemed on Friday so that he could go out decently dressed on Sunday, but not always.

If goods were not redeemed after a certain number of weeks, the pawn broker would sell them to anyone lucky enough to have a job and some money to spare. Anything of any value was pawned in those difficult days — watches, jewellery, rings, crockery and bedding. Anything that could keep the wolf from the door.

Father liked to cheer us up sometimes with stories and sayings. If anyone asked him how he was he'd say, "I'm fine. The trouble is, everything I eat flies to my stomach."

And there was the tale of his grandmother's cat which was getting so old they decided to drown it. "But that's a terrible thing to do!" I was horrified.

"That night when we went to bed, we put the cat in a tub of water with a brick around his neck..."

"Father!"

"And in the morning we found that the cat had drunk the water and was sitting on the brick, safe and sound."

He was a great one for pulling our legs, was father.

Chapter 9

When I was fourteen I left school. "You have a good reference," the Headmaster said. "Try to get into an office."

At the time, this was absolutely impossible. There simply wasn't any office work available, not unless you knew someone of influence.

Nearly every day I used to trek down the hills to the Education Committee in the hope of finding such a job — without success.

Many months later we heard that the Automatic factory were taking on young girls. Along with about fifty others, I got the job there. The first morning Alf took me on the tram to work out the best way of getting there.

The job entailed putting nuts into a small machine that buzzed round to receive them. When we didn't get it exactly right, it hurt the fingers. At the end of a fortnight we all got the sack. I wasn't sorry, it wasn't a very nice job. Telling May, an older friend, she said, "That's not right, sacking you. When we have a Union they won't be able to do that."

After this, I started applying for jobs in shops, but was always told, "Come back when you've grown a bit." So that was no help.

Liverpool was full of factories in those days — Barker & Dobson, Tate & Lyle, Crawfords, Jacobs, Lybro — who made overalls, Shinio Polishes, Ogdens and Gallaghers Tobacco Company, a pen company and the British American Tobacco Company where I eventually found a job.

One of the old ladies from down the street was a Matron at the B.A.T. as it was called. She put in a word for me. Even with a big firm like that and so many vacancies, one had to come with a recommendation.

On being given a job there, the first thing that happened was vaccination. Everyone working there had be vaccinated. The doctor had an instrument with two prongs with which he scraped the skin until it bled, not once, but twice. He then introduced the cow pox vaccine to the wound. For the first time in my life I fainted.

The scars didn't heal the way they should have done and for weeks I had to have them cleaned and dressed by the factory nurse until mother said, "Tell them you won't be going back to them for the dressing. I'll do it for you." And so she did, using Robin Starch, and at last the vaccination healed.

The first day at work with B.A.T. I was put on brushing. I worked from 8am to 6pm. I ached from head to foot and arrived home exhausted and went straight to bed.

"She can't keep that job," said mother, "it's too much for her."

"She'll get used to it." said father.

So I kept at it for nearly 12 months. Being one of the last batch to have been taken on, it was the same rough brushing work. I also had to see to the fire buckets, emptying them every so often and refilling them. They were hanging on hooks and it was difficult to reach them. The first time I upset one, and it drenched me. "It's not good enough." a couple of the older ones said, "She shouldn't have to do that."

In the Stemmery — which some called the Stripping Room — it was dusty and hot. The leaf tobacco was the only important thing there. "The 'eads are comin'," we were told by the Section Head when the top manager was due to come round. Everything had to be spic-and-span so that even before he'd set off from home we were prepared for his inspection.

It wasn't us that he was interested in or the conditions we were working in. No, his only concern was for the tobacco leaves. "Shut these windows!" He'd say. "Turn up the humidifier."

The humidifier was a wide pipe which ran the length of the room sending out warm moist air, making the environment even hotter, even more unbearable.

Sometimes I'd sweated so much that without any Amami or other lotion, my hair was sticky enough to set — with sweat! At night, before going out, every item of clothing had to be removed to get rid of the strong smell of tobacco.

Snobbery was rife in the factory, as well as outside. Office and shop workers were a cut above factory workers, even though we got more money than any of them. Fourteen shillings a week was the pay, 14/- for 8am to 6pm five days a week. Imagine!

In the factory itself, Section Hands hung their coats in one part of the cloakroom, the forewoman in another part. We christened ourselves the 'common herd', though strangely enough, no one had ever questioned this practice until I came along. At home, we'd always been told we were as good as anybody else, so I'd been brought up with strong democratic ideas. Even as we laughed at ourselves as the 'common herd' things didn't change much. In the dining room for instance, those with any authority sat apart from the rest of us, considering us beneath them.

But there was an Under-Foreman I was friendly with. We rode to work on the same tram. He was a tall man with fair hair and a lovely complexion. He always smoked and coughed all the way home and later died of consumption.

Working conditions were terrible. Not only did we work in a cloud of tobacco dust, but everywhere we went the air was thick with smoke – tobacco smoke.

Nearly all the men smoked, starting it as soon as they were old enough to buy them. Some sneaked a fag from their dad's pack and smoked in secret. The saying was that they smoked behind the bike sheds in school, from the age of about twelve. But very few women smoked. In those days the campaigns were all about alcohol and not tobacco.

The one bright spot in my life at this time was that Lily was working at B.A.T. too, though in a different department. The Rose Packing they called it. Some of us went there when a special order had to be despatched at short notice.

In the Rose Packing, things were so different from conditions in the Stemmary. Here there was no dust and the atmosphere was clean. The transfer usually only lasted half a day, and then it was back to our normal environment. Back to hell.

The people who stayed for dinner couldn't leave the factory in the dinner hour which made it a long dreary day. Lily and I decided to sneak out and eat our sandwiches in a small park nearby, which was mostly deserted at that time of day. We never told anyone about this. It wasn't the thing to do, eating outside. We managed to keep this up for a long time until one of the girls questioned us.

"I thought you said it was too far for you to go home at dinner time?"

"It is. We go to somebody's house."

"Whose house?"

"You don't know them."

"I might."

"Well, we're not telling you."

"Why not, eh? D'ye think she'll tell someone?"

"She's so nosy." Lily said, "She won't give up until she finds out."

"We'll stay in then, until she's forgotten." I said. "We won't go to the park for a couple of days."

And that's what we did. But it was awful staying inside, along with everyone else, with the dusty atmosphere and the smell of tobacco. From eight in the morning until six at night without a break, without a breath of fresh air. It was so awful. It seems silly now, looking back, but that hour out of doors made such a difference. She spoilt it for us, that interfering girl.

We could have gone home for our dinners but by the time we got there we'd only have had ten minutes before we had to set off for the factory again. It wouldn't have been worth it.

"You going to the park tonight?" Lily asked one day.

"Yes, we're going to have a rounders match with those boys. It's a shame you can't join in."

"Yes it is, but I've got work to do."

"Don't the boys do anything in your house?"

"No, they're like little tin gods."

"It's the same with us, but Dolly and Edie are there helping mother while I'm out at work."

"Alice and May are moving, did you know?"

"No I didn't. Who told you? It's a bit sudden isn't it?"

"My mam said someone saw a policeman going to the house and taking their dad away."

"Why?"

"Because he's a bookie. And betting's against the law, isn't it?"

"Is that why they're going then? Why they can't stay here?"

"I believe so. See you tommorrer. Tara!"

Once a bookie had been raided, he always had to move away from the neighbourhood.

❧ Chapter 10 ❧

Queenie had re-married and had two boys. She was very poor. Her husband was a busker playing the violin. This wasn't allowed on the dole, although quite a few men did it, playing in pub doorways.

At night, men from the U.A.B. (Unemployment Assistance Board) went around to catch them, so that their dole could be stopped. With three boys to keep it was a struggle for her. Mother helped her as much as she could. One day, she brought Bunty, Queenie's son by her soldier husband, home to live with us. He was a real handful, quarrelling with his Uncle Albert, who was younger than he was.

The other two boys told their mother, "We don't like going to Grandma's because Aunty Flo always washes us." Well I thought they needed it, they only lived in one room.

Queenie had managed to get a house a few doors away from us. She did a lot of knitting to help out financially. She taught me to knit. The first thing I made was a vest which turned out rather big. "That'd fit Nell Moonie," she said. Nell Moonie was a very big woman!

The church had a football team and some of us girls went to watch them play, both at home and away when they could pay for a room in a house on a Corporation estate to change into their football gear.

On Bank Holidays we all went to New Brighton, walking along the 'prom to West Kirby and walking back the country way to board the boat at New Brighton for Liverpool. The boats were always full, and we often had to queue for the next one.

One time, we went to Thursaston. We were just sitting down to eat our sandwiches when there was a commotion and shouting – the weather was so hot the hill was on fire! The boys helped to put it out and were taken into one of the houses afterwards to get cleaned up.

"You should see it!" They said. "A bathroom and a lavatory upstairs!" A coupie of them lived in two up-two down houses. We all arrived home happy, the boys delighted at being acclaimed as heroes. They couldn't wait to tell everyone.

The Grand National was run on a Friday then. The Sunday before was Jump Sunday when the public were allowed to go round Aintree Racecourse to view the jumps. Now, on Friday, it was the big day.

Lord Cunliffe-Owen, one of the Directors of B.A.T. had a

horse in the race so we were given half a day off (unpaid) to go and watch it. "I hope his horse falls at Beecher's Brook." Somebody said on their way there.

The road to Aintree was crowded with people, on the pavements and in the middle of the road, dodging cars and taxis, surging forward as they were joined by others along the way. All were eager to reach the Melling Road before the gates were closed. The view was better from that side. It was the best place to be to see the race for nothing.

Back to work on Saturday morning, everyone was talking about the race. "Did his horse win?"

"No it didn't!"

"Oh, poor man, he must have lost some of his wealth."

"You're only jealous."

"Well, aren't you?"

"There's too much talking." The boss called. "Get on with your work, all of you."

"The day I'm leaving, I'll say plenty to him." Muttered Alice.

We only worked until one o'clock on Saturdays. Mother was busy ironing when I got home. "That girl from over the road called for you, Flo." She said.

"Which girl?"

"The one who looks as if a good feed would kill her."

"Oh, you mean Sarah."

Sarah didn't have many friends. She'd been educated at a small private school. She dressed well.

"All the money in that house goes on her back," neighbours said.

"Pigs in clover."

"Who do they think they are, paying out for a private school?"

"Venice Street School is as good as that one."

"I agree with you, Mrs T."

Albert loved animals. When the cat was missing at night, we knew where to find it — in his bed! he went to the park one day and brought home a box full of caterpillars. Next morning, they'd escaped from the box in the kitchen and were all over the place. We spent a couple of hours collecting them from the curtains, the dresser and the chairs.

He had a snake called Sammy which used to find its way to the coal place in the yard. Going out there for a shovel of coal, sometimes something would rear up covered in coal dust. Sammy came to very sad end. One day Edie and I happened to be passing when one of a gang of men who were clearing the drains held up the stick he was working with. There was Sammy dangling from the end of it.

"Be careful, it might bite."

"It's dead, isn't is? Stone dead."

We broke the news to Abbie. He was upset.

"We'll get you another one." Alf said.

All the back yards had high walls separating them from each other. Most houses had a cat and they would parade round on top of the walls. Those that were let out at night fought with one another, making a terrible row, until someone went out and threw a bucket of water over then. It was quite usual to see cats with bitten ears and parts of their tail missing. Still, they earned their keep, as most houses had mice.

One day, the two lads were busy white-washing our yard walls. "That looks a lot better," Mother said. " Much brighter." It made a difference to the look of the place, all freshly white-washed. Somehow the plants om the window ledges suddenly looked more colourful too!

"There's talk about electricity," Alf said. "Electric lighting instead of gas."

"Be a long time before it come here."

"It's up to the landlords to have it put in."

"It'll mean they charge us more rent."

"Well, at least we'll save on gas mantles." These were quite expensive and were always being broken or burning out. There was a knock at the door. I answered it. "Who was it?" Mother asked.

"It was that fella selling gas mantles, wasn't it."

"Any gas mantles today, Polly?" he asked in a sing-song voice.

"Strange, just when we were talking about them."

"Oh, I saw him coming," Alf said. "I saw him down the street, that's what made me think of it, gas mantles and electric lighting." Alf had recognised the gas mantle man.

When more young ones started at work, I was moved to what they called 'the tables'. These were the bins that held the tobacco leaf to be stripped. Each bin was closed in on two sides, and on the third there were two conveyor belts, one above the other, to take away the leaf that had had the stems removed.

We did this work, sorting and stripping the leaf tobacco, with a thing called a thimble which dug into the thumb. My thumb is still mis-shapen from wearing the thimble. It was such monotonous work, that, with the heat of the place, it took me all my time to keep awake. But the quota of stems stripped had to be kept up.

The tobacco came in huge hogsheads and was first separated into trolleys by the men and then taken to the end of the conveyor belts and thrown on top by one of the girls, to be picked up by those working on the table.

As we stripped the stems from the tobacco, the bottom belt carried away the leaf, while the stems were put in a basket on the other side. I always liked a high stool so that I could talk to a friend when the boss wasn't watching us.

One day, the monotony was relieved by first a shout, then a commotion. Among the leaf tobacco being flung onto the belt

was a nest of live rats. People were jumping around and screaming. men with brushes were banging them to drive the rats away.
We'd all seen rats in the factory before, of course, running up the
wall and along the rafters, but this was altogether too much,
certainly for the girls — though the men took it all in their stride.

When I told them about it at home, mother said, " She can't
stay there." Dad said, "She'll have to. Jobs are hard to get.
Besides, it's good for her to learn how to mix with different kinds
of people."

He was right, of course. For instance, I'd never known any
Roman Catholics before, but in the factory, I had made many
Catholic friends.

From the history books, I knew all about the Battle of the
Boyne. I knew that Liverpool had always had parades to commemorate it, and there were frequently fights and this and other
anniversaries of the Irish struggle for independence. But these
marches were nowhere near our area. They had nothing to do
with us.

"That Mrs D gets on my nerves." I said.

"Why? What's she done?"

"There's no pleasing 'er. She's just asked me when I'm going to
stop growing. Before it used to be 'When are you going to start

growing?'"

"She's only showing she's interested."

"Well, I wish she wasn't. There's nothing I can do about growing, is there?"

"You weren't rude to her, were you?"

"No."

"Don't be."

I'd have like to have told Mrs D to mind her own business, but I wouldn't have dared. Adults always felt they could say whatever they liked to young people, but we couldn't answer back.

"Going out?"

"Yes, I'm going to the baths."

"She's mad on swimming, our Flo." Edie wasn't.

It was salt water in the Westminster Road Baths, and there were two pools — one for the males and one for the females. It was tuppence to go in and everyone had to wear a swimming cap.

"As you go, chase that jigger rabbit off the wall, Flo." Jack called. A jigger rabbit was what we called cats.

I met a few of the gang at the baths, and on the way out we arranged to go to a Spiritualist meeting together. It was very funny. The woman told different people things about themselves. She kept throwing her arms around saying, "Och awa!" as she pushed away the spirits who were clamouring for her attention. Or so she would have us believe! We were at the back of the room trying to stifle our giggles.

"There's a disruptive influence among us today," she said, "I can feel it."

An accomplice of hers came and ushered us out. "She's a fake." we all decided. " A good job we didn't pay. We'll go to a real medium one day."

We all wanted to know whether we'd get married. That was all the future held for us girls in those days. Girls like us. The only alternative was to stay single and become a teacher.

"I wouldn't marry anyone who got drunk." I said.

"Come on, they all drink, don't they? Some of the women even go with a jug and fetch the beer for them. All men drink."

"I've seen the women going down the entry to the pub," Maggie said. "Mrs R from down the street puts a man's caps on to go to the pub."

"You know everything!"

With that we separated, Lily and I to go home. "I can't be late in, or I won't be up for work in the morning."

"Me as well. Dad'll be watching the clock as usual."

Uncle Alec was talking to father as I went in. He was the husband of my mother's sister, Net (Henrietta). They had another sister called Tot (Florence). Thank goodness nobody ever called me Tot!

"There's talk of a general strike. Will the workers at your place be coming out?" Dad was asking Uncle Alec.

"I suppose some will turn in, yes." He managed a large printing firm. "It's very bad everywhere. In Jarrow they're getting up a march to Downing Street."

"I'm sure the strike will happen. The Government will have to do something then. The people are starving. Giving Relief Coupons doesn't help much. It's money people want. Jobs and a living wage."

The strike did happen. Some women drove the lorries to get the factory products distributed. They weren't very popular mind, though many of them were promoted when it was over.

The one thing that stayed in my mind was the night my friend Chrissie and I went to Margaret Street Baths, the only swimming pool that remained open.

"I don't like fresh water," she objected. We'd always been to salt water swimming baths.

"Oh come on, don't be a spoil sport."

"I'm afraid there's no heat on," the attendant said.

"That's all right. We're not worried about that."

An empty swimming pool all to ourselves. Imagine! Chrissie jumped in and came straight back up the steps shivering. The water was freezing. I swam a length and had to be helped out by the attendant.

"Better have a hot bath when you get home."

That was a joke. By the time the back kitchen boiler had been lit and stoked and the copper filled with water, I'd either have frozen to death or have thawed out again. It just wasn't the trouble. No wonder nobody was swimming in such dreadfully cold water!

Chapter 11

By now, the family tent had been exchanged for a small caravan. We'd go off at the weekend and on Saturday night we'd usually walk over the fields to Moreton. Mam and dad would go into the Farmer's Arms for a drink, but children weren't allowed in, of course, so we'd wander around and make our way slowly back to the caravan. By then, it was usually just the three of us, Albert and Edie, with me looking after them.

This particular weekend, they were back from the pub early as mother wasn't well. We took the train home next morning, and she went to bed and stayed there for a while, but she wasn't getting any better and in the end the doctor sent her to hospital.

As a baby, Albert had been a worry to them. He'd been delicate and needed a lot of extra care and nursing. At this time, mother was just starting to get her strength back. She had even begun to go out with father sometimes and enjoy herself. She'd even bought herself a pair of dancing shoes.

But now she was ill again. The doctor said her heart was strained. And, after a few weeks, the hospital said she had consumption, or TB as they call it today.

She was anxious to get back home so that she could keep an eye on us all from her bed. Dad bought a bed-chair that she could lie on during the day. "I'll be better downstairs." she said, "Where

I can see what's going on."

Every morning before I left for work, I'd lean over mother to see if there was any change in her. And the same at night. But she wasn't getting any better − our mam was getting worse. In fact, she was dying. She couldn't manage the stairs any longer but had to be carried up and down. I knew I must keep checking that she was still breathing. Every morning I expected to find that she'd died in the night.

The girls at work were sympathetic. One day they kept saying, "You all right chuck? You look terrible."

"Yes, I'm all right."

When I got home, I said to Dolly, "There's something wrong with me. I've got pains in my stomach and I'm bleeding."

"Come upstairs," she told me. After rummaging in a drawer, she threw a square of terry towelling at me and a belt and some safety pins. "From now on, you'll have that every month." she told me.

"All my life?"

"Yes, you'll get used to it."

I had to ask Queenie what it was all about.

"You're lucky," she said. "Sixteen's late to start."

Mother was getting worse and worse. We crept in to see her when we could, but by this time she was unconscious. After a week of this, Alf called us altogether and said, "It can't go on like this. By going in all the time, we're keeping her back, keeping her with us. From now on, Dolly will look after her during the day and I'll stay with her at night."

For the next four nights we kept vigil around the table. Jack's girlfriend was with us too.

On the last night, we heard movement in the bedroom as we sat at the table. She had gone, pour soul. Father went upstairs. When he came down he told Edie and me we could go up.

The bedroom was dark. Mother was lying there with a bandage round her jaw and a penny on each eye. I ran out. Alf followed me and put and arm around me. "You shouldn't have gone in yet." he said. "Later she'll look better."

The undertaker came and put her in a coffin. The curtains were drawn shut. The mirrors were covered in black. I went into the parlour. She looked peaceful now but so thin. Her chest was so small, like a baby's.

Neighbours kept coming in to see her. Caroline came in to the kitchen to talk to us. She looked all round and said in a tearful voice, "She's leaving a lovely home," and had us all crying again. I suppose to her, our house was so much better than her own miserable place.

Until the day of the funeral, Edie and I went to stay in the house next door. The nice neighbour brought us breakfast in bed, toast and marmalade. She had no children.

All of us went to the funeral except Albert. We were all dressed in deep black. The funeral coaches were each pulled by two horses.

I had nightmares for a long time afterwards. I dreamed I was riding in the funeral coach again, sometimes on the top of it, throwing soil onto the coffin with mother looking on. Terrible nightmares. Poor mother.

Afterwards, because of the TB, we all had to go and have a medical examination. I had signs of trouble. My chest wasn't clear of it.

Without mother, the family seemed to go to pieces. Father left everything to Dolly. At the Memorial Service she was so upset she had to be taken out. Dolly took charge of the caravan and the bit of money that over the years mother had struggled to save. She treated father very well, and he thought she was wonderful.

There were always arguments. Father always took Dolly's side. Edie and I sometimes ganged up against her, but it was always me that got the blame. Edie seemed to be able to slide out of trouble.

Father still took notice of everything that we did wrong. The day I got my hair shingled, for instance, I kept my hat on for fear he would see it.

"Take your hat off in the house."

"I'm going out now."

Next day I'd forgotten about it, when a loud voice thundered, "Whatever's the matter with that girl's head?"

"It's a shingle."

"The sooner it grows the better. Don't get it cut like that again."

"I like it."

"Well I don't. From the back you look like a boy."

So that was that.

"You might have known dad wouldn't approve of it," said Dolly. "Are you going to the Social tonight?" It was the Church Social.

"Yes, we are," Edie and I said together.

After the Social, father was waiting for us. "Look at that clock!" It was ten o'clock. "It's far too late for you to be out, you two."

We shuffled up the stairs leaving him muttering to himself. "Wait until I see Miss Wallace. Keeping girls out till this hour, indeed!"

"Wasn't all that good this time, was it?"

"We had a laugh when George stood up."

"Except that we knew what he was going to say."

"Yes, his usual – "Stand up, speak up. And shut up. I've done the first two, now I'll do the third.'"

"He says it all the time, that's why everyone laughed."

"Last in bed puts the gas out."

"Leave it on Flo. Dolly'll be up soon."

Edie's birthday came at the end of the month. Father gave her the usual big apple, and we made duck apple for Albert. It wasn't a happy occasion, nobody's heart was in it. Christmas too would soon be here, and what would it be like without mother?

As it happened, it didn't turn out too badly. Being at work made a difference. The girls included me in their conversation now, although most of it went over my head.

Most people paid weekly for the things they bought. There seemed to be a Club for everything – a Christmas Club, a Photographic Club, Clothing Clubs, Tontines. My shilling a week didn't allow for any of those.

At work, my first experience of Christmas Eve on the tables, was a huge 'doorstep' sandwich coming down the conveyor belt for me. I immediately passed it on.

Dolly had never gone out to work but had learned to cook from mother. This year Dolly made the Christmas bunloaves and Edie and I took them to the bake-house. After the family dinner I begged for Lily to come for tea. Her mother agreed reluctantly. Jack and Mary supplied a small tree for the table, with a few little presents on it.

"Thank God we got through that all right." Alf said.

"You girls have worked hard." dad said. "You can leave the dishes till morning." What a concession! We'd been up early for Abbie, trying to make Christmas good for him.

Edie left school at Christmas. "I'm not goin' in a factory." she said.

"It was good enough for me." I said.

"But look at you, coughing all the time."

"It's only a cold she's got. She'll get over it."

Plates

The Sunday School 'Big Treat' at Halewood

*The caravan —
where we spent
many a happy
holiday*

*With younger
sister Edie, after
she got her glasses
— which she hated!*

*Angus the Scottie dog —
bought for me by Les, after
our family mongrel died.*

Here we are with the
Welsh Miners' Concert
Pierrot whom we met
while on holiday

And this is me
on his knee!

At New Brighton Baths one glorious summer. We loved to sit in the fountain and let the cool water rush over us!

I wore the costume I spent ages knitting on this occasion. It had a swallow on the front and the obligatory skirt!

We loved playing tennis in the park courts. It cost us sixpence each and this was the fashion in the 1930's

Ella and I shared many holidays over the years. Here we are enjoying one of them in August 1929

This is me aged 22 in our back yard with the wringing machine

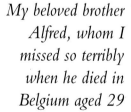

My beloved brother Alfred, whom I missed so terribly when he died in Belgium aged 29

*The Sunday School
treat at Parbold*

*My elder sister
Dolly and Ernie,
her husband, on
holiday at the
caravan*

This is the second medal I won in Venice Street Public Elementary School

It was awarded in 1921 for

'marked regularity of attendance and general good conduct during four years'

"Well, it's not for me I'm telling you. I'm not going to the factory, I'm not."

So Edie had her own way again, as usual!

There were two kinds of people we were involved with; those who went to Church and those who had stopped going. Edie mixed with the second crowd, the one's who'd been thrown out of the Band of Hope.

"Don't you think it's funny?" she asked me.

I suppose it was funny sometimes, like the Sunday the superintendent heard munching and said, "You boys come out and put your carrots on the platform!" We all laughed at that.

I had two friends who were 'only children', neither of them had any brothers or sisters. They both lived in big houses. Molly always wanted me to go round to her place. She never came to our house. Her mother was a lovely person. The other one was Hilda whose father managed a big shop in town and Hilda worked in the office. Her mother gave wonderful parties.

"Are you goin' to Hilda's party?" Dolly asked.

"Yes, I am."

"You'll have to take her a birthday present."

"I know, I've already got her one."

"What is it?" Edie wanted to know

"I'm not telling."

"I don't care. I don't want to know. I don't even like Hilda anyway."

"Stop arguing, you two."

Edie started work in the greengrocers at the end of the street. She was serving one day, when the customer said, "What's your name?" When Edie told her she said, "I'm related to you by your father's first wife. She died in childbirth."

Edie came home raging on about it to me. "Didn't you ask her anything more about it?"

"No, I'm not goin' to speak to her again."

"I'd have tried to find out more."

"You would, but not me. I'm not askin' her anything."

We didn't dare mention it to any of the rest of the family. I don't think they ever knew. "I don't believe it." Edie kept saying.

"Why would she say it then, if it wasn't true?"

"But mother was ten years younger, I'd guess. Ten years!"

When we were alone in the house we searched everywhere for clues, but to no avail. Even today, the matter of father's first marriage is taboo, a well-hidden family secret.

Dolly, one of my friends at work, told me her brother would like to go out with me. It was all arranged very properly. She invited me to her house to meet George. We went out together for a few months. He was a nice boy, but dull. I was reading romances and going to the pictures, so I had a clear idea of what was to be expected in the circumstances. But George never even held my hand!

Chapter 12

Money was so short that in an effort to keep the teenagers off the streets, they'd decided to open the schools for evening activities. Plays and pantomimes were popular, and over the years, I was in all of them − Cinderella, Puss in Boots, Dick Whittington. I knew most of the parts in each production and can still reel them off today.

With mother gone, Dolly was in charge of the household now and it was very hard to get any money out of her for anything. Even for necessities. When my shoes had holes in the soles, she said, "I can't afford to get you a new pair, not yet. Put cardboard inside until I can afford to buy you some more."

It was no use asking father. he left everything to Dolly. The only thing he worried about was us being in on time at night, and making sure we were up early in the morning before he went to work at seven o'clock.

I always had a cup of tea before I left for the factory, and took a slice of bunloaf with me. That was my breakfast. "This bunloaf seems to be going down." Dolly said to Edie. They both knew it was me. Edie wasn't keen on sweet stuff.

"It's supposed to be eaten, isn't it?" I said.

"Not as quick as that, no."

"I'm not the only one in the house. Why're you blaming me?"

I went on cutting myself a piece on the sly until it was all gone.

An Evangelist from America came to Liverpool. Pastor Jefferies he was called. On one of the large playing fields on Stanley Park a huge marquee was erected. Every night, crowds gathered inside and out. Pastor Jefferies was a faith healer and people staggered out to the front for him to put his hands on them and heal them. Afterwards, many of them threw away their crutches and sticks, claiming they had been cured.

After a week, the whole contingent moved to a piece of waste ground. They were happy to pitch their tents anywhere the authorities allowed them to. Wherever Pastor Jefferies went, crowds followed him, probably hoping that he would work miracles and improve their lives.

Twins we knew finished up with religious mania and were put away in the asylum. In spite of this, Pastor Jefferies was a wonderful preacher, and a very nice man.

Our Section Hand at work invited him for tea. "Come and meet him after." She said to me. And I did. Whether those he touched stayed converted or stayed cured, only those near to them know. I cannot say.

Since starting work before mother died, I hadn't done any housework, but now, under Dolly's strict eye, before going out at night, the beds had to be made and Edie and I took turns washing the dishes.

"I'm in a hurry tonight." Edie said one evening. "Will you do them for me?"

"It's your turn, and there'll be cabbage pans." We hated cleaning the cabbage pans.

"There's only one cabbage pan."

"Oh, all right."

She dashed out, leaving me with a load of dishes to wash and four pans. When she came in I tackled her about it.

"You said there was only one pan."

"No, I didn't. I said there was only one *cabbage* pan."

"You won't catch me out like that again." I said. "Next time, I'll make sure I know what I'm letting myself in for."

But Edie only laughed.

"For goodness sake go to the doctor, Flo." Alf said one morning when he came downstairs. "You've kept me awake all night, coughing. Even when I managed to doze off I could still hear you. Cough, cough, cough. You must do something about it."

"I'll go tonight." I said.

"See that you do."

So, after work, I went to see the doctor.

"You've got bronchitis." he said. "Can you leave that job? The dusty atmosphere in that factory isn't going to help you."

"No, there aren't any more jobs."

He knew the circumstances. "I'll give you a note to stay off for a few days. And one for the insurance people too."

That was important. Without a doctor's note, there'd be nothing coming in. It was no work, no money. If you got a sick note, the rules had to be obeyed or the insurance company wouldn't pay up either.

No going out after six o'clock was one of the rules. They were always looking for defaulters. Any excuse to avoid paying up. They employed snoopers too.

Dolly wasn't pleased. She urged me to get better, to get back to work as quickly as possible. That was only the beginning.

I used to have what was called a summer cold. One day it got so bad the Welfare Officer at the factory sent me home. When I got there, nobody was in, so I made a poultice of tea-leaves, drew the curtains and went to bed. Dolly came home and the first thing I knew was that she was shaking me, saying, "Wake up! Wake up! Whatever's the matter with you?" The poultice had slipped off my eyes and my face was covered in tea-leaves. "I thought you had some dreadful disease." she said.

Edie came upstairs. "You didn't half give her a fright."

"I didn't hear her come in. I was asleep, wasn't I?"

"Are yeh comin' down then?"

"I suppose so."

"You go to the baths too much," father said when I got downstairs. "You go out too often. No wonder your nerves are bad."

I'd have liked to have said, "My nerves are bad because now that mother's gone, you get drunk, dad." But I couldn't. Even Edie wouldn't dare to say that to him. Not that she minded. They took it for granted, Edie and Dolly, and just tried to avoid waking him up from his drunken stupor. He was always bad-tempered when he was drunk.

He wasn't really an alcoholic, our dad, it was just that he couldn't take his spirits. And it was spirits the ships' captains gave him when they invited him into their cabins for a quick one.

When he hadn't been drinking, he was thoughtful and entertaining. Albert would beg him for a story sometimes. "The one about the corn ..." We'd sit around the fire and he'd begin:

"It was a dark and stormy night and the rain came down in torrents. There was a band of brigands. The chief brigand said 'Antonio, tell us a tale, man.' Antonio began as follows; 'In a far and distant land, food was becoming scarce, so the leader of the people built a huge barn and filled it with corn in case of famine. But for a tiny space high up in the roof, the barn was full of corn. Quite full. One night a bird found its way into the barn and took a grain of corn. And another bird and took another. And so it went on.'"

"How did it end?" we asked father.

"I can't tell you that until all the corn has gone!"

Dad was very popular with the church folk, reading the lesson at evening service. "You're a street angel and a house devil." mother once told him.

Talking in a group one night, a woman was complaining about her aches and pains.

"I'll give you a cure for them." said father. "Get a pint of milk, boil it down to a quart and make pills out of it. Take one after you go to sleep at night and one before you wake up in the morning and you'll be as right as rain."

The woman was so fascinated that it didn't sink in at first. "Oh, Jack!" she said. "I thought you were serious."

"Cured your pains for a while, didn't it − until you worked it out."

Caroline accompanied us home that night. From then on, she was a frequent visitor, especially when dad was home. "She'd like to be your second mother." A friend said.

"She won't get anywhere with our dad." Dolly said fiercely.

"Is my overall ready, Dolly? It's work in the morning."

"It's washed. You'll have to iron it yourself."

It was such a chore, ironing. Heating the flat iron on the gas, having to spit on it to check how hot it was. Sometimes the hot spit ran right down onto your arm and you'd have to put a dab of flour or oil on it to stop it blistering.

At B.A.T. we were supplied with two white overalls, one on and the other in the wash. Every Monday it had to be clean overalls. When it was very hot, some of the girls just wore their overalls with no dress on underneath. One night an order came round that overalls must be left in the workplace from then on.

"Do they think we take tobacco leaves home with us, then, hidden under them?"

"It's them searchers, giving themselves a thrill."

I didn't really know what they meant. The searchers were a team of tough women who did body searches as we left the factory each night. Frisking they call it today, running their hands all over our bodies. Heaven knows what they thought we could be pinching from the tobacco leaf department!

Because of the protests, the boss relented and allowed us to keep our overalls on and go home in them that night.

Lily met me as we came out of work and we walked home together. "Can you come to the pictures tonight?" I asked her. "I've had to stay in all this time with my cold."

"I don't know."

"I'll call for you, anyway."

"All right then."

Lily's mum opened the door. "You're not going out like that are you?"

"Why not?"

"That dress you're wearing, it's not decent."

It was a sleeveless dress. "It's the fashion."

"I hope I never see you wearing one of them, my girl," she said to Lily. "I don't know what things are coming to. It's not decent."

"Bye, mam!"

The picture we saw that night was Dracula. We were so scared that we walked home in the middle of the road for fear of what might jump out at us from a dark alley.

When I got in, I was sitting on the sofa waiting for the others to go up to bed, too scared to go up on my own. But I fell asleep, and they turned the gas out and left me there in the dark, alone. I had to scramble up the stairs and jump into bed without a light.

In the middle of the night, Abbie had a nightmare and started screaming. "It's got me! It's got me! Aah! Aah! It's got me!" I'll be the next I thought, lying there stiff with fright.

It didn't stop me reading horror stories mind. And ghost stories. But not only these, among other things, I managed to read the Origin of Species!

A Jehovah's Witness persuaded me to buy a book at the door called The Watchtower by Judge Rutherford who was the leader of the movement at that time. His book proclaimed that Rutherford would be 'taken up', but in due time he died in the ordinary way. That was the end of it for me, my faith was shattered.

"My shoes are still leaking." I told Dolly. "If you give me back a bit more from my wage packet, I will keep myself." She agreed.

The first thing I did was to join a clothing club at work and they gave me a coupon which I could use in a shop to buy a pair of shoes, paying weekly. Now I'd make sure my shoes wouldn't 'let in' again. In future, my feet would stay dry whatever the weather!

Chapter 13

At last I was back at work! "The boss wants you," said Alice. I went to the desk.

"Can you add up?" he asked.

"Yes, I think so."

He gave me a long column of figures to add up, to test me. "That's right, now these two." I got them right too. He explained the system to me.

"*Gross* is the weight of the trolley filled with leaf. *Tare* is the weight of the empty trolley. If you take one away from the other, you get the weight of the leaf which is the *net* weight." These three columns had to be accurate. "Would you like to work on the desk?"

"Yes!" I was delighted. The girl who had been there all the time was called Ella. She was a bit stand-offish at first, but we soon became very friendly. I loved the job. It meant I was now able to go all round the factory in between the trolleys coming through to be weighed and recorded.

Ella had only one friend, Annie, a school teacher. I got through pencils very quickly because I always worked with a very sharp point. Ella had to order the pencils. She'd say, "You had a new one a fortnight ago."

"I don't like a small pencil."

"You'd think she was buying them herself," Alice grumbled. "She's just the same with me."

The thing I particularly liked about me new job was telling the girls how much bonus they'd earned. If anyone was late in the morning, the time would be deducted from the bonus. If they were late, they had to report at the desk. They'd say, "My mother is sick." They didn't like telling their excuses to Ella – they knew very well she didn't believe them. So whenever they could they came to me.

"She should get up earlier in the morning," Ella would say. "She's just lazy, that's her problem."

"You don't know what they have to do before they come to work," I'd say, trying to stick up for them. Ella had it easy. Her mother cooked her breakfast for her, and she only lived few streets away from the factory. "If you were on bonus payments you wouldn't like to lose them." I told her.

"I don't suppose I would."

"Besides, you have to put down what they tell you, whatever you think. It isn't really anything to do with you."

She agreed reluctantly. I knew she felt superior to those who came from a different background, I could sense it. But it wasn't long before we were going out together.

A friend of mine asked me to go to her wedding night party. "And you can bring Ella if you like." When I told her we'd been invited to Eva's party, she wasn't keen at first. But I soon persuaded her.

"She lives in Bootle, doesn't she?"

"Yes, but I don't know where exactly."

"All right then I'll come with you. It's a long way for you though. You could stay at our house, if we're late getting away."

Now it was father I had to tackle. It would help if I could catch him in a good mood, so I chose my moment carefully. "Where is this party?"

"In Bootle."

"That's a long way away. How will you get home?"

"Ella said I could stay at her house. She lives near there."

"All right, but make sure you're home in time for Sunday School."

The party was a disappointment. The six roomed house was overflowing with people. They were in the hall, sitting on the stairs, in the bedrooms, as well as downstairs. We stayed a couple of hours before wishing Eva "Goodbye!" for once you were married, that wa it.

No married woman was allowed to work at the tobacco factory. Those who married secretly, to try to keep their jobs, were soon found out and given the sack right away. It wasn't only B.A.T. that did this. It was common practice in those days.

Leaving early like that, I could have easily have got home that night. "You're not going home after all, are you?" Ella asked.

"No, I'm not." I stayed at Ella's and never mentioned it to any of the family.

"What was the wedding like?" Edie was curious as usual.

"Very nice. Lots of people there."

"Did yeh stay long then?"

"Yes, we did. And then we went back to Ella's."

"You were gone when I got home."

Edie worked in a different greengrocer's now. It was a long way away. She worked so late on Saturday nights, she had to get the last tram, and it was sometimes midnight when she arrived home.

"What's the house like? Ella's I mean?"

"Very quiet. It's tidier. And they don't quarrel like we do here. There's only four of them. Her father and mother are very nice. And she's one brother a lot younger than her. Ella doesn't have to help at all. Her mother does everything in the house, everything."

There *were* quarrels in our house. I suppose it was my fault sometimes. I had such a good memory that when something was mis-quoted I had to correct it. If someone was embroidering a story, I always had to challenge them. And that caused arguments, of course. Somehow father always seemed to blame me.

Queenie had moved into a house a few doors away. Her husband often refused to give her any money for the rent or anything. She'd come and tell Dolly sometimes, and Dolly would go and make him cough up. That was when they were pally, Queenie and Dolly. Other times, they didn't speak to each other. Dolly was sulky. Queenie was fiery. Watching all this, I swore to myself that if ever I got married and had a family, things would be different. My husband wouldn't be allowed to carry on like Queenie's.

This was a time when for once, we were all on speaking terms. On Saturday afternoons when the men went to the football match, we four girls would sit together and knit and natter until it was time to get the tea ready. The evening meal had to be on the table when the men came in, or there'd be trouble. The rest of the weekend was spent arguing about the match. About the teams and the goals and the result.

One of the times when Queenie and Dolly were friendly, Queenie asked if she could have some of mother's clothes. "I'll give them to you when I see your own things looking shabby." Dolly said. Queenie never got them. She could have asked dad, but she didn't. Difficult as things were for her, she still had her pride.

That visit of mine to Ella's was the first of many. If we went to the picture's in Bootle, say, we'd go back to her house afterwards. "You're always welcome here." her mother told me.

At Easter, we went away for a weekend, Ella and I, to Hope, a small village on the fringe of Wales. Ella had been there before.

For the trip, she had dresses her mother had made, all the same style but in different colour material. Her mother had packed for her. I had two jumpers and one dress. No skirts however, I'd forgotten to put one in the case.

The son of the house and his friend took us round. "Would you like to see the Blacksmith's shop?" Glyn asked one day.

"As long as I don't have to go near the horses."

"I'm surprised at you," he said. "I thought you liked animals."

"I do, I love them. But horses are a bit too big for me. I like smaller animals, like your Toby." Toby was his dog.

Seeing us on the train together, Glyn said, "How did you two get together? You're so different, like chalk and cheese."

"We're good friends."

Later on, we went to Hoylake for a week's holiday. Ella's friend, Annie, came too. "I can only stay until Friday," she said.

We bought our food and catered for ourselves. We came in one night laughing. The landlady met us on the stairs. "When you two were here before, you were nice quiet girls. It must be you that's making them so noisy." she said, looking at me.

On Friday when Annie was leaving, she cut herself a piece of our cheese. "I'm taking my share." she said.

"What a funny woman," I said.

"She gets holiday pay, she's lucky." We certainly didn't. "I'm glad she's gone," I said. "She's too staid for us."

"I wonder what she'd have done if we'd eaten her cheese?" Ella said.

"Probably never have spoken to you again. Come on, let's go out."

We went out laughing.

Chapter 14

King George V and Queen Mary were coming to Liverpool for the opening of the Gladstone Dock. The Union of Girl 's Clubs choir had been practising for weeks, getting ready to greet their Royal Highnesses with patriotic songs such as Rule Britannia, Hearts of Oak and Sons of the Sea.

At work, to encourage as many people as possible to attend the ceremony, we'd been given a holiday (unpaid of course!). Waiting for their arrival on the Royal Yacht, we were split up, boys on one side of the dock and girls on the other,

Into the third verse of Rule Britannia, there was a stir among the crowd. "They're comin'" But it was a false alarm. A sailor's hat was floating merrily around the dock. A boat was lowered. A man went down the steps and rowed across the dock to the cheers of the spectators, to rescue the hat. He made it back safely and the singing resumed.

After a while, there were murmurs again. "They're comin'". It was another false alarm. "What's happening?" The ribbon the King was going to cut had been broken, it was trailing in the dock. Once again, the intrepid boatman launched the boat. This time, he went down the steps and retrieved the ribbon to the applause and cheers of the people lining the docks, those at the back craning their necks and pressing forward to find out what was going on.

"They're late. They were supposed to be here half an hour ago."

"We've been here for ever!"

Suddenly, the sound of cheering floated on the air. This time, the royal party really was coming. The Royal Yacht sailed into the dock, gliding gently into place with scarcely room for it between the harbour walls. The King in full dress uniform and a chest full of medals saluted the boys from his side of the deck. On our side, the Queen, resplendent in jewels, acknowledged with a dignified wave, the cheers of te assembled girls — and that was it really.

After the long wait, the ceremony was all over in what seemed a few minutes, and we were on our way home again. "Did you see the Queen? They say her face is enamelled."

"I wouldn't be surprised. She never smiled."

"Frightened she'd crack it, the enamel."

"Was it worth it, all those hours we waited?"

"She was so near, I felt I could have leaned over and touched her."

"You won't see them again, that's for sure."

But she was wrong about that. We did see them again, years later when they came to open the Queensway Tunnel under the River Mersey. On that occasion too we waited for hours for a glimpse of the King and Queen. Once the ceremony was over, we were allowed to walk through the tunnel to Birkenhead. We walked to Birkenhead, *under the Mersey*. Imagine!

When we reached the far bank, we turned round and walked back again, thousands of us, walking through the Mersey Tunnel. It was a long trek, especially after we'd been standing around so long beforehand and we still had to walk home afterwards.

"It's terrible when you see all their jewels," someone said as we walked home now from the Gladstone Dock. "They must be worth a fortune."

"It's terrible when you think that most of us can't even afford the tram fare home."

"Aye, it's time something was done about it."

There was such a contrast between the splendour of the royal party and the shabbiness of the people watching. Folk who'd waited hours for a brief sight of them, as I had.

At work the next day, I was suddenly doubled up with pain. They sent me to the Welfare, to lie down. There were two beds in Welfare. I lay there all afternoon, listening to the throb of machinery from the factory. Then they sent me home with instructions to go to the doctor.

As usual, Dolly wasn't in when I got home. (I wonder where she used to get to all the time?) I went to the surgery on my own and the doctor told me it was appendicitis. "You'll have to go to the hospital," he told me. "I'll send and ambulance for you."

The ambulance son arrived. Dolly was back by this time. "There's an ambulance outside," she said.

"It's for me."

"I can't come with you. I've got to get dad's tea."

I realise now that the hospital must have thought I was some sort of waif. I had to remove all my clothes which was painful for me, as in our house we'd never been allowed to come downstairs in an underskirt, certainly not when any of the men were around. I sat there for hours waiting to be examined, naked under the hairy blanket. All alone, of course.

I was kept in a week. Dolly came at visiting times, though she usually only arrived five minutes before the bell went at the end of the visiting hour. I didn't have an operation then.

"You've got what's known as a grumbling appendix," the doctor told me.

Lily had not been to the opening of the Queensway Tunnel. "No wonder you're ill," she said. "All that standing, all that walking."

Then it was Lily's turn to be ill. When I called for her, her mother said, "she can't go to work, love. She's ill."

Coming home that night, it was a shock to see an ambulance drawn up outside Lily's house. "It's pneumonia," her mother told me.

"Pneumonia my foot!" Alf said. "That girl's consumptive." He knew about these things, Alf did, having been in hospital himself. He'd had a couple of operations too.

It turned out that Alf was right. Lily was transferred to Broadgreen, which was the TB hospital, for consumptives. She went through some awful treatment, poor Lily.

I used to go and see her every week. They tried all sorts on her. One week she was really breathless. They'd collapsed one of her lungs.

One Sunday, Eide went with me to Broadgreen to see Lily. While we sat there talking to her, she kept her hands under the bed clothes. Edie kept looking at her in a funny way, and, as Lily brought a hand out from under the sheet, Edie fainted.

"What happened?" we asked her as she came round.

"It's her hands, Lily's hands, they're black." Edie said.

"That's the ointment silly. The treatment gave me a rash. The ointment's for the rash. Black ointment. Edie never went to see Lily again.

Broadgreen was always grim, but winter in there was even worse. One snowy day I went out to visit Lily and there she was lying on an open veranda. There was a light covering of snow on her blankets, and birds fluttered down beside her hoping to be fed.

Lily was in the TB hospital for five years. "Will you go and see Lena?" she asked me once. "Tell her where I am." Lena was a cripple in a wheelchair. Lily used to take her out, pushing her round the theatres and picture houses. Not all of them allowed a wheelchair in, but Lily would usually manage to persuade them to let them in.

She would miss these outings and their visits to a film or music hall or play. Even her own sister, who was good to poor Lena, didn't go to that much trouble for the crippled girl.

At any time I was unable to visit Lily, I wrote to her — letters and cards. One day Lily received a letter from me. Handing her the letter, the nurse said, "You've been in here so long that they've changed your name and they're calling you after the hospital now!"

Instead of Miss Lily Broderick, what I'd written on the envelope was Miss Lily Broadgreen!

Chapter 15

Every Tuesday evening, Ella and I went for a walk in the park and listened to the band playing there. One night just as I got off the tram I met Ted, one of the gang I'd been friendly with. "I've been waiting for you." He said.

"Haven't seen you around for ages," I said. "Where've you been?"

"I joined the Air Force. Will you come out tonight?"

"Sorry, can't come tonight."

"Tomorrow then? Just for a walk and a talk. I'm going back on Wednesday, then I'll be posted abroad."

"All right then, tomorrow night."

Now what would I tell Ella? Usually if I was meeting one of the boys she came too. But this time I wanted Ted to myself, so I made some excuse to her and met him as arranged.

He was in his Air Force uniform. At that time, Airmen were still so unusual that people in the street stared at him. A couple of girls from work came by and said hello. "You told me you weren't going out last night." Ella said.

"Yes, but I happened to bump into Ted, and as he was off again today, we went for a walk."

She gave me a funny look as much to say she didn't believe me.

But she didn't actually say it. I felt bad about it and thought of the text hanging in our bedroom that said;

'Be sure your sins will find you out.'

I should have told her straight. Next time, I decided, I will.

One day, coming home from Sunday School, where I was a teacher now, I stopped for a chat with some friends. Dolly came along. "Don't forget, it's your turn to make tea tonight, Flo," she said as she passed me.

"She's not your sister, is she?"

"Yes, she is."

"Well, I wouldn't have thought it. You're not in the least alike."

Afterwards, Dolly asked what they'd been saying. I told her.

"That cobbler said something to me about it," she said, sounding very annoyed.

"It's not my fault. They said they knew Edie was your sister but didn't think I was from the same family. They thought I must have been adopted."

"Don't talk so soft! You're like mother. You take after her."

I knew this was true because there was a huge photograph of mother on the wall. I could see how like her I was. Both Dolly and Edie resented it. It was nice to rub it in!

One night, when father was feeling jovial and talkative for a change, Dolly said, "I'm your eldest daughter."

"And I'm your youngest daughter," said Edie.

What could I. say? "I'm just the one in the middle"? I said nothing and kept on reading.

"What yeh reading?" Edie asked, looking over my shoulder.

"It's called The Girl of the Timberlost. It's about a girl whose father was lost in sinking sands and her mother tried to save him."

"How excitin'"

"I want to finish it so that I can tell the girls about it in the morning."

"I thought you said you weren't allowed to talk at work?"

"The boss can't watch everybody all the time."

It wasn't always like that between us, quarrelling and picking fault. We'd go out together sometimes, Edie and I. Sometimes with Dolly as well. Chattering away as right as rain. Laughing and joking if we saw anything that struck us as funny.

Like the time we were in the tram and this lady stepped on with an enormous feather standing straight up from her hat. We were sitting on separate seats trying not to look at one another or we'd have burst right out laughing. Out loud.

And the time in Lewis' store when we were watching a

demonstration of an 'unburstable' balloon which burst when someone touched it. Not liking to offend the demonstrator, we rushed around the corner and laughed ourselves silly.

In Church one Sunday, the congregation all seemed restless and whispering together. "What's happening?"

"We've just heard the Scripture Reader is leaving."

"That's a terrible shame," people were saying. "Mr Bidston's so popular."

"Yes, we'll never have anybody as good as him, that's for sure."

"The new man won't make any changes," they said, announcing Mr Bidston's departure.

They were wrong. The new man came and after his very first sermon, he told the congregation that the mission was closing. In future we'd be expected to go to the Big Church. "They'd always been jealous up there of the attendance here."

"Who is the new man, anyway?"

"Mr Medhurst."

A few people did transfer to the mother church, and some to another C of E. Others went to the Weslyan Church – but not all of us. In our family, father took us girls to the Methodist Chapel. Since he joined the Army, Jack didn't go anywhere any longer and Alf was already a Superintendent at the City Mission.

The Methodist service was just like the Mission's. We had hymns, a reading, a sermon. I'd already learnt the Catechism in the Church of England, though there were parts of it I strongly objected to, such as promising to 'order myself lowly and reverently to all my betters'. Who were my betters? Not some of those who would probably claim they were.

'To do my duty in that state of life into which it has pleased God to call me.' I wanted something a good deal better than the state I found myself in, thank you!

When father stopped going to church, we kept on – Dolly went with her friends, Edie and I with ours. We used to rush home to the lavatory in the back yard. Father had put a notice on the door;

'Surgeon'

After a few weeks of this, another notice appeared;

'Short bright services, don't over-crowd. Overflow meetings outside'

One Sunday, coming out of church, it was teeming with rain. Edie and I ran all the way home with our straw hats under our coats because it was better to be drenched that have a lump on your hat. If ever one of those straw hats got wet, it somehow bulged up in the middle. It had happened before, more than once – that's why we were wise to it. It didn't matter about us getting wet, but we couldn't keep discarding straw hats. A hat cost money.

"The baths have opened again," Betty said. "Will you come with me tonight?" She was a keen swimmer too.

"I think my cap's perished."

"I'll lend you one." Betty was a girl from school. She always had two of everything.

"All right. Meet you at the bottom of our street."

The baths closed in winter, opening only for galas. "I believe you won a race at the B.A.T. club gala."

"Yes, I did − a pair of bookends."

"What's up with you?" one of the older girls asked me at work the next morning. "You're walking like an old woman."

"I went swimming last night − I'm aching all over." It was always the same, the first swim of the season.

"Rather you than me."

Father was sympathetic. "It's the muscles that haven't been used for a while. It's agony, I know."

"Did you do any sport when you were young, then, dad?"

"I did some roller skating. In fact, I was a champion roller skater."

I couldn't believe it. Roller skating! Our dad! He was over 70 now. He'd always been old, as far as I could remember. Our dad roller skating!

Chapter 16

I had heard that the lady who ran the Sunday School with her daughter had left St Cuthbert's. I met them one day, they were always together.

"We didn't get along with Medhurst. We've opened a new School. All the old pupils have come with us. Will you come and teach again? You would be welcome to join the Concert Party too, if you'd like."

"Oh yes! Yes, I would like that."

"Come along tomorrow night for an audition, a try-out."

For my piece, I sang Land of Hope and Glory. "That's fine," they told me, and I was accepted as a member of the choir.

The first concert we gave was at a refuge for homeless men, run by a philanthropist called Lee Jones. He was what you might call a 'real gentleman'. Everyone who met him endorsed that view. "Mr Jones is a real gentleman," they'd say.

We went to many places with the choir, to a home for old sailors, to any clubs trying to raise money for charity, and our usual Christmas concert. Once, we even went to Winwick, a large institution with rows and rows of men and a guard at the end of each row.

I spoke to one of the guards, asking why they were there. The men looked all right to me, decent enough, sober.

"Well lass, you might say you're the Prince of Wales. Right. But when these men say they're the Princess of Wales or the Prime Minister they really believe it. That's the difference. These fellows are insane, that's what."

"What a shame."

"They have to be kept locked up for their own sakes, or there's no knowing what they'd be getting up to. Prime Minister, indeed. Napoleon Bonaparte. Julius Ceasar. We've got them all in here, you know.

I was thankful we didn't go wo Winwick again.

In our little group, we were thrilled when the new swimming baths were opened in New Brighton. We couldn't wait to try them out.

"Weren't you knitting yourself a new costume?" Kitty asked. "Did you finish it?"

"Yes, I did."

"What's it like then?"

"It's got a swallow on the front. And a skirt." Skirts were compulsory then.

"You'll have to watch it doesn't fly away," said one of the boys who fancied himself as a comedian.

Another one had to chip in at that. "What'll yeh do if it starts comin' undone eh?"

"Don't worry, it won't!"

We arranged to go to New Brighton on the Saturday. "Remember to take your Number Two Brownie camera."

"Right-ho!" Ben liked to talk like Tom Merry from the Greyfriars School stories.

The new baths were wonderful, with fountains playing and seats in tiers for spectators – and, an incredible innovation – mixed bathing for the first time!

We each had a turn sitting on the edge of the fountain with the double jets giving us a cooling shower. "Say cheese," Ben called out, and we grinned into the camera.

"It's a bit different from West Minster Road Baths."

"And Balliol Road." The water was awfully salty there.

"I didn't know you went there," said Tom.

"She's in the Everton Ladies Swimming Club. That's where they meet, Balliol Road."

It was hard to open your eyes when you came out of the water at Balliol Road, it was that salty.

At work, I was friendly with a girl called Minnie who entertained some of us with lurid tales of the men she had been out with who 'tried it on', as she put it. I didn't believe her myself until one night on the tram a man followed me upstairs.

"I've paid your fare," he said.

"Thanks very much, but you needn't have bothered." I was very innocent.

"It's all right, I'm a friend of Minnies."

"That's no recommendation!"

"I'm perfectly respectable."

When I got off the tram, he followed me. I started walking away, but he was still following me. I stopped and faced him. "What do you want?"

"No need to get like that. I just want to take you out. That's not much to ask, is it? Just this once?"

"I don't go out with men I don't know."

He was a handsome devil, and so darned sure of himself, so certain he would win me over. We stood there arguing, but I wasn't going to be caught out that easily. In the end he gave up and went away.

"How did yeh get on last night, eh?" Minnie asked at work next day.

"What do you mean?"

"Didn't you go out with Stan?"

"Who's Stan?"

"A friend of mine. He boasts that he can get any girl. Easy."

"Well, he didn't get me, I can promise you."

"We had a bet on it, that he'd persuade you to go out with him. He's lost that bet by the sound of it."

"Listen Minnie, I can spot a wolf a mile away."

"he is a wolf, you're right. He's the one who pulled all the buttons off my blouse."

"Well, thanks for setting this wolf onto me, Minnie. You're a great friend."

"Oh, I knew you'd be all right. He needed taking down a peg. You probably taught him a lesson."

I'd been staying in a lot, practising Alf's songs with him. I knew them all by know – songs from the Australian Bush, Indian Love Songs, Negro Spirituals and the Classics of the day such as Jerusalem and The Last Chord.

One night, Alf came home full of excitement and told us he'd been offered a job as a manager.

"Are you taking it?" Dad asked.

"I certainly am. With work so scarce, I'd be mad not to."

The job Alf had been offered was in Brussels, Belgium. "Are

you sure you're up to it?" I asked him. After his operation Alf had been very ill. He still wasn't fully recovered.

"Don't worry about me, Flo. I'll be fine. It's a great chance."

he was to go next week. As soon as that. "You'll write to me, won't you?" he said. The next week! My heart sank.

"Yes, I will," I said, the tears rolling sown my cheeks. "I'll write every week."

"Don't be upset, Love. I'll be coming home on leave every so often."

I missed Alf terribly. He'd always been so good to me, especially after mother died. It was Alf who had taught me how to deal with people, how to look after myself at work and out in the world. And he'd always encouraged me to read, not just novels. To use the library and read widely on every subject, which I still do today.

I wrote to him every week, as I promised I would. He lodged with a Belgian lady whose daughter worked at the Palace Hotel. Along with other English men working abroad, Alf eventually became a founder member of Toc H which gradually established clubs all over Europe.

he only came home on holiday twice. When he did we could see he was being looked after better that at home. His suit was beautifully pressed, the frayed cuffs of his shirt were well-darned. I was very proud of this handsome brother.

In his letters, he was always eager to catch up on the news of course. About how Everton Football Team were doing in the league, and all. In one letter he mentioned how he'd like to hear from Dolly.

When he wrote that he wasn't well, I was very worried. he said he might not be able to write so often, not until he was better, "but please keep writing to me," he said. "You're the only one who bothers."

A few weeks after this, he wrote to say that this would be the last I would hear for a while – he'd write again when he was better. I grew more and more anxious.

Then, a letter came from Belgium, asking if one of us would go out to Alf as he was now dreadfully ill. Jack and Dolly went. They were met off the boat by the landlady's daughter. "He wait for someone," she said. What she meant was that he was hanging onto life, knowing his family were on the way to him. He was hanging on to say goodbye.

Two days later a telegram came telling us that Alf had died. I was devastated. If only I'd been the one to go over to be with him at the end. In all the time he'd been in Brussels, Dolly had never even bothered to write to him. And yet it was Dolly that went to see him at the end. It was very hard to bear.

Jack and Dolly came home with photographs of the funeral, which had been very elaborate with plumed horses, and everybody following the coffin in a long procession. All the houses along the route to the cemetery were draped in black, they told us.

"Why didn't you write to him more often?" I said to Dolly

afterwards.

"I did. I did write to him," she said.

"You didn't," I said, and showed her the letter in which he'd mentioned it.

"It's no use talking about it now," father said. He was right. There was no point in talking about it. Alf had gone. My dear brother Alf. All I had to remember him by was a handkerchief of Brussels lace that he'd sent me. That and his letters. It was 1932. I would never see Alf again. He was 29 years old, my lovely brother Alf, and I would never see him again.

ᒼᔕᐣ Chapter 17 ᒼᔕᐣ

I was in the doctor's waiting room. When it was my turn he called, "Come in Floradora."

"You're well in with him," a friend said.

"Yes, he came every day to see my mother." When she was dying.

When I wen in through to the surgery, the doctor put out his cigarette in the ash-tray. "You've got bronchitis," he said. "I'd like you to be x-rayed." And he arranged an appointment for me.

After I'd had the x-ray and went back to see the doctor again, he said, "It's not consumption, I'm glad to tell you. Dr Jackson is the best specialist we have."

The doctor from work sent me to a Convalescent Home in Woolton. It was right out at the tram terminus, which in those days was a long way out of town. Interviewing the newcomers at the Home, the Matron told me to stay behind.

"Yours is an unusual name," she said. "Do you have an uncle who owns a saddler's shop?"

"Yes, I believe I do, though we've never met him."

"I used to go out with him," the Matron said shyly.

After that, she was always very friendly with me but very strict with the others.

"You're her pet," they'd say.

"It's not *me* she likes, is it? It's my uncle."

Behind the Convalescent Home, a path led straight into the woods, between an avenue of huge trees. As it was winter, the trees were generally shrouded in mist and the cawing of crows sounded weird.

"It's creepy," I said. "It's like the setting for a ghost story."

"I'll show you something even more creepy," said Elsie, who'd been in the Home longer. "Come on." And she led us to a secret bower. "There used to be a seat here but it's been taken away."

"Why?"

"Because there was a murder out here. An American soldier killed a girl ..."

"Let's go back and sit by the fire, Elsie."

When we got safely indoors, someone said the Matron wanted to see me. I knocked on her door.

"Come in," she said. "Don't look so scared, you're not in trouble. Do you like it here Florence?"

"Yes, Matron, I do."

"We have a very nice time here over Christmas. Would you like me to get you an extension? So that you can be here for all the Christmas jollifications — parties, carol singing, special food and all — would you?"

So that's what happened! I stayed in for Christmas and we all had a really wonderful time. They even let the men join us for

Christmas Day.

Normally we were kept strictly apart, the men and boys in another part of the building.

A Convalescent Home in West Kirby was very different. The Matron there was religious. Every night there was a short service for staff and patients. The Matron spoke in a loud deep voice.

"Give yeh the willies," the girl next to me said.

"How about that lace cap she wears?"

"Be quiet!" Matron thundered.

In the Common Room, there was always fierce competition for the seats nearest the fire. There was strict pecking order about this. As one patient got up and left, the next one moved in to take her chair.

"D'ye think we'll ever get a turn near the fire?"

"Be thankful you're living."

This conversation, and others like it, was carried on during the two hour rest period. Each afternoon, we had to rest properly on our beds. It was all right for the older women, but we young ones didn't like it. For one thing, during the rest period we weren't supposed to talk.

With so much unemployment, there were many itinerant showmen trying to make a living. They'd turn up on the waste ground with placards announcing their skills. Their tricks! One man who fancied himself as the 'New Houdini' used to ask a volunteer from the spectators to tie him up in chains, put him in a sack and then tie the sack tightly shut too.

Unfortunately for him, on one occasion the man who stepped forward was an old 'sea dog' who tied the sack so tightly the prisoner couldn't escape from the sack and the crowd quickly melted away. Eventually his cries of "let me out!" attracted the attention of a patrolling policeman who had to release the poor fellow.

Another time, there was a man who sold watches for a shilling. One of te lads bought one, but although he kept shaking it hopefully, there was no tick, no sign og life in it. So he wriggled his way through to the front of the crowd again, and handed the watch back to the salesman.

"Not goin' eh?" he said, taking the dud watch and holding it up for them all to see. "Just wind it up with the ball of the thumb," he said, and holding it in the palm of his hand, he demonstrated the winding technique. "Wind it once, twice three times," he said loudly. Then bending down, he said in a menacing voice, "Beat it son, just you beat it."

When the boy opened the back of the watch, it had no innards, no working parts. The watch case was just stuffed with newspaper. And the man had already disappeared. You had to be careful with those showmen and salesmen. You had to keep your wits about you.

The fair came to Sheil Park once a year. Some of the stall-holders were regulars, coming back year after year. The man who sold medicine for kidney complaints always attracted a crowd.

"Is your water dark and cloudy?" he'd shout in a loud voice. "take a bottle of this and I guarantee it'll cure you. If it comes to the knife, God help you!"

There must have been many folk suffering with their kidneys – his bottles of medicine soon sold out.

Another man offered a cure for corns. "The cure will work right through your boot!" he'd shout. To promote this wonder cure, he displayed a disgusting collection of corns that had dropped from people's feet thanks to his potion, or so he said. He offered to remove corns there and then, for free. One man couldn't wait. He was already sitting in the operating chair with his shoe off and his socks rolled down exposing a hairy leg, eagerly waiting for surgery.

The worst fraud of all was the man selling fly-catchers. He had a rotten cod's head on show, but no flies went near it. Afterwards it was discovered to be soaked in paraffin oil. As the fair was lit by paraffin flares the smell wasn't particularly noticeable – especially against the stink of bad flesh.

I once won a coconut, but when I got home, I found it was bad. Nevertheless, it was all good fun. All the fun of the fair! While it lasted. Until the wagons and vans pulled away and left Sheil Park quiet again, all the noise and excitement over for another year.

Sometimes a fair would come to another park in another part of the city. Sometimes they were grander affairs altogether, with Hobby Horses (called Hurdy Gurdies in those days) and a cakewalk. And perhaps a Carousel with clockwork figures beating time to the music, with their heads twisting backwards and forwards as it turned.

The coconut shy seldom had to hand out any coconuts. "They're stuck on with glue," people used to say in disgust.

Once, coming away from the fair, we did see a man carrying a coconut. "Have you won that?" he was asked. He said he had.

"By jove, you must have muscles like Elmo Lincoln!"

"Who is Elmo Lincoln?" I asked, telling dad about it later.

"He's a noted strong man."

No wonder then, that he won a coconut!

Chapter 18

"I'd like to go to the caravan this weekend," I told Dolly.

"We're not going this week. You can't go by yourself."

"Three of the girls from work will come with me."

"You'll have to pay."

"That's all right. They said they would."

"I mean you as well."

"Mother bought the caravan for all of us."

"Well, it's mine now and if you aren't prepared to pay, that's it."

I did pay and we did go.

The caravan had three rooms, including a bedroom with a big bed in it. There was a bed in the kitchen too, but it had to be made up at night and cleared away in the morning. The first night, after lighting the fire and sitting round it for a while, we decided we'd all like to sleep in the big bed. Renie had the bright idea of sleeping widthways on the mattress. It wasn't really wide enough though. In the middle of the night I awoke to find my legs dangling down outside the blankets.

"Wasser matter?" one of them muttered, which woke the others. We re-arranged ourselves and soon were all sleeping cosily, lengthways on this time, having decided to fix up the bed in the kitchen for the next night.

The caravan had been moved to Sealand, a village outside Chester. At the top of the lane was the River Dee, very narrow at this point, with a one-man ferry boat plying backwards and forwards from our side to a little place called Saltney on the far bank.

"Shall we go swimming tomorrow?" Mabel asked, as the ferry took us over to Saltney where we'd get fish and chips for supper.

The ferry-man overheard this and said, "Yer want to be careful, swimming hereabouts. The currents are very strong. When the tide comes in, you could be swept away. It's mighty powerful the River Dee."

"Why's that then?" I asked him. We'd never heard of this danger before.

"It's called a bore – right. The water comes roaring up the river. Foaming up, higher than a man above the bank. Depends on the moon and the tides, the bore. And the time of year and all. There's one due about now. Just you be careful now. It's not safe to go swimming just now."

We found out when it would happen and went to watch it from a safe distance. It was a wonderful sight. First we heard the roar of the water, then the tidal wave came rushing up stream, the water higher than the land. In a few minutes it was all over and the river floated peacefully again in its bed.

I can't think why they call it a bore! That's the last thing it was, boring! It's something you never forget, witnessing the bore roaring up the River Dee.

Back at work again, back in the heat and dust of the tobacco factory, we were separated, each to her own job. It seemed a long way from the green fields and the river and the easy days together of our caravan holiday.

"We're getting a wireless set," I told the girls.

"Lucky you!"

"It's my brother's. When I got home from Cheshire, there it was with a huge battery that had to be taken to the shop every so often, to be refilled with acid. Recharged I suppose. The set had a crystal in it and a thing called a cat's whisker that had to be twiddled about on the crystal to pick up the sound, and a pair of head-phones so we could only listen one at a time.

The big bands were very popular then. Sometimes I'd just get home in time to hear Henry Hall playing 'Here's to the next time', which meant the programme was over! What I wanted to catch was his signature tune 'It's just time for dancing'.

Frantically twiddling the cat's whisker to improve reception and make it clearer, I used to learn the words of the songs for the girls at work. But sometimes it was hopeless and no matter what I did to the cat's whisker, the music would fade away completely.

In the news bulletins, we heard that the scientists were trying to split the atom. They'd been trying for years we were told.

"Everything is going to be different now," said father, when they at last achieved their goal. "Everything is going to be wonderful."

But what have they actually done with this amazing break-through? Made a bomb that killed thousands, even if it did help to end the 'war to end wars'. As far as I can judge, not many blessings came from the splitting of the atom.

By this time we had electricity, which we could boast about to those poor people who still had to rely on gas lighting in their homes with the endless problem of broken gas mantles. Electricity was sheer heaven. Compared with candles and oil lamps and finally gas lighting, imagine how wonderful it was going into a room and just clicking a switch!

When the Mormons came to Liverpool it was like an invasion. They came for a week and set up their headquarters in Blair Hall which belonged to the Co-Op. For that week, on every street corner along Walton Road stood these lovely looking young men, eager to persuade us all to go along to the Mormon meetings. We went every night, my friends and I. Their accents reminded me of Sam and Ben, the two American soldiers I had been so fond of years before, when I was still a child, and the war was still raging.

I wondered about them, Sam and Ben. I wondered whether they were still alive, and whether they ever thought of their friends in Liverpool.

The Mormons told us that they came from one of the lost tribes of Israel. They also insisted that, no matter what we might have heard to the contrary, they only had one wife apiece, like everybody else.

The climax to their Liverpool mission was a special meeting on the Sunday afternoon. Their placards said

All Welcome

Of course, we went along. We wanted to see these handsome young missionaries at close quarters. But what a disappointment! None of the bright-eyes young preachers were there, only a group of withered old men performing some sort of play which was supposed to win us over to their faith.

As far as I could gather, the play was about the first Mormons and how, by their own shining example, they somehow atoned for the sins of their non-Mormon ancestors.

We came away with a pamphlet picturing some of these worthy souls, all of whom were descended from the saints. After the mission, when most of the Mormons had moved on to their next port of call, a few stayed behind and kept up the pressure on us, going round from door to door, trying to convert us to their way of thinking.

The aim was to open a Mormon church in Liverpool, but I don't remember that anything came of all their efforts. They didn't make any converts. We certainly weren't won over.

After the Mormons had gone, everywhere seemed so quiet, so

dull. Queenie had moved away by this time and Dolly was in complete control of the household. She had somehow managed to organise a house exchange, though it only took us to the other side of the main road, three doors along from the church.

It was a very large house, the new one, with two sitting rooms, tow good bedrooms on the first floor, and three more in the attic. Now, for the first time, we could spread ourselves out. There was a bathroom in this house, with a lavatory. In the basement were the kitchen, the back kitchen and larder, with another lavatory outside up steps in the yard.

Now, in my attic bedroom, my own attic bedroom, I could read to my heart's content. The only snag was a flight of stairs outside up to the front door, which had to be scrubbed daily, and mostly by me.

Edie had a habit of always wanting to use the bathroom the minute I had settles in for a good old soak.

"Hurry up," she'd say, banging on the door. "I want to come in."

"Go away, can't you — I'm in the bath and I'm not moving. Leave me alone. Go downstairs."

"I know what you're up to — you're readin' in there, aren't you?"

I was reading, it's true. It was so quiet and private in the bath, floating in the hot water, with a towel to rest my head on. It was sheer luxury. Especially after the tin bath in front of the fire that we'd had until now, and having to heat the water and fill the tub and clear it all away afterwards. And having to choose a time when the boys were safely out of the house and would be out long enough. The boys, and father too.

Compared with that, it was absolutely great now to be able to have a bath whenever we liked, in our proper bathroom with water coming hot from the taps. For me, always coming home from work smelling of tobacco, it was a particular blessing, our new bathroom.

That tobacco smell was so insistent, it clung to your clothes no matter how often you washed them. It lingered in your hair and even seemed to permeate the skin. Tobacco!

August came, and our annual holiday from the factory. Most of the girls went to the Isle of Man. Ella and I went to Wales and stayed on the outskirts of a small mining town. If the coal wasn't being mined fast enough in the eyes of the owners, they'd close the pit and all the men would be out of work.

The people were desperately poor and nearly starving. They used to sneak coal waste and any odd bits of coal they could find from the outcrops and the slag heaps around the mine, just to keep a fire going in the miserable little pit houses they lived in.

Visiting a seaside town during our trip to wales, we went to a concert on the pier given by a group of miners who had been laid off in this way and were trying to make a living with pierrot acts and cabaret for the summer visitors. They were all very friendly in spite of their desperate situation.

We became very involved with them during that holiday. Sometimes they invited us up on the stage to join them in the good old music hall choruses.

I felt rather sad for them. We weren't well off ourselves, but at least we were working, we had our wages coming in every week. These men were keeping themselves going in this cheerful enterprising way, but come the winter, what would they do?

We put what we could in their collecting box, but we hadn't much ourselves and we had to keep enough in our pockets to get us back home at the end of the week. I can still see those miners who *were* working coming away from the pit at the end of their shift blacker than the coal they mined.

Apart from the fairs, there were other events that we looked forward to during the year.

Once a month, the Boys Brigade marched round the streets before church on Sunday with a brass band leading the way. As they passed us, the watching children sang along to whatever tune was being played;

> *'Here comes the Boys Brigade*
> *All covered with marmalade*
> *A tuppence hapenny pill box*
> *And half a yard of braid'*

On the 12th July, the Orangemen paraded in front of the people on their way to the Sunday School day out to Southport. The Roman Catholics used to wait in the lower quarters to try to break the ranks of those in the band. Sometimes they threw pepper. It seemed to be all part of the fun. Many of us went to watch.

On that Sunday they paraded with the pipes and drums playing before going in to a service to commemorate the Battle of the Boyne in 1690. Fanatics on both sides have gone now. The struggle between the Orange and the Green was a feature of life in Liverpool for hundreds of years.

Many people visited the Chinese community in Pitt Street, especially at the time of their New Year celebrations when their streets were decorated with colours that we didn't see every day, brilliant reds and golds.

On Empire Day, the children vied with one another to trim their bikes with the best red, white and blue decorations. Shop windows were gaily dresses and flags flew everywhere. This was a joyous day to celebrate the ending of the war, but the next commemoration that came around in November wasn't happy at all.

The two minute silence on Armistice Day, when we remembered those killed and wounded in the war, was a very sombre occasion. And, with nearly every family having lost someone, a son or husband or father, it was taken very seriously.

So many men who *had* returned from the trenches were too crippled to work again. Thousands of others had had their lungs ruined by mustard gas and had little hope of ever finding a job.

"The Government will have have to do something," father kept saying. For us, the first signs of the problem affecting those who were working was the closing of the other Liverpool B.A.T. factory in Leeds Street. Some of the Leeds Street workers were switched to jobs at our factory, of course. And we suddenly had a new foreman who had transferred from the other factory.

"Watch out for him," one of the section hands who had transferred with him warned us. "He's a horrible man."

I soon came to agree with her opinion. We seemed to have a surfeit of bosses already and this one wasn't needed. I was walking down the room one day when a loud voice behind me kept shouting, "Ey you!" Ey you!" I knew who it was all right, but I ignored him and kept going about my work.

"Didn't you hear me calling you?" he said, running after me.

"No, I didn't. I heard you shouting though. 'Ey you' isn't my name, so why should I stop?"

He was livid but there was nothing he could say and he went away and reported me to the head of the department who sent for me afterwards and, having listened to my side of it, shook his head. "That's all right," he said. "I don't think we need take this any further."

I thought he agreed with me about the awful man, although he couldn't actually say so. After this, Mr Bishop, the senior boss smiled whenever he saw me, though he didn't come out of his office very often.

The others were delighted. "Well done, Flo. You did him one in the eye and about time too." "It was certainly time somebody stood up to him."

He was nothing but an ignorant fellow using long words to impress us, but as often as not using them in the wrong place or the wrong sense. It ws quite amusing at times. And a small victory for me!

Chapter 19

With my next bout of illness, the girls at work kept calling to see me. An older girl, Mary — I didn't like her much but she was kind over this — had taken up a collection round the factory for me.

"I don't know why you're so darned popular," Dolly said. "It isn't as if you've got blue eyes ..."

"Are you jealous then?"

"Jealous! Of course not. Why should I be jealous of you eh?"

There was no answer to that.

I got to know this Mary very well after that. She almost seemed to be trying too hard to be my friend.

"I just wanted to get to know you," she told me, explaining why she'd organised the collection. I was flattered, of course I was.

"I don't like that sister of yours though," she said.

"Oh, she's all right. We still play rounders together in the park, me and Dolly. She's not as bad as she sounds."

Sometimes when we were playing in the park, some of the boys who had their own games going would make up a team with us and we'd all play together. It was friendly and fun.

As the nights began to draw in, two of these lads took to

walking home with Dolly and me, afterwards. Before long, they asked us to go to the pictures with them.

"We'll have to ask dad," Dolly said gloomily.

"Where is it you're thinking of going?" he said. "Which picture house?"

"The Queens in Walton Road."

"What time does the picture finish?"

"Quarter to eleven." We'd known he'd ask this and checked.

"That means you should be back here by eleven o'clock. right?"

In spite of the cinema piano players being drowned out by the Salvation Army Brass Band practising next door, we enjoyed the film. As we reached home, the door opened and there was father waiting for us.

"Get in," he said, and leaving the lads standing there, we followed father indoors. I was 17, Dolly was 20 and we followed him in like two little lambs.

"We're not likely to see those two again," said Dolly. But before long we bumped into them in the park. For fear of father they always saw us home by ten o'clock. Gradually they were allowed into the house and father began to accept them. Dolly's boyfriend was called Ernie. Mine was Frank.

Ernie soon made himself at home with us. If there were jobs to be done, but he and Dolly were going out, he'd say, "Let them do it," meaning Edie and me, as if he had a say in it.

I went out with Frank. Sometimes we'd play tennis with his sister and her boyfriend. And afterwards we'd go back to their house where his mother always made me feel very welcome. He took me to football matches. We'd go in the stands, where there were no proper seats but rough benches made from planks of wood. It was friendly and informal.

We'd all be mixed together, our team's supporters with the supporters of the opposing team, with no friction between us. It was perfectly good natured and cosy. We'd go to watch Liverpool one week and Everton the next.

When we went to the pictures, Frank would buy a box of Cadbury's Dairy Milk for us, but he'd always get it from the cut-price shop for eleven pence halfpenny, instead of a shilling. It was a silly little thing, I know, but it began to annoy me, him and his cut-price chocolate.

To be honest, he was beginning to irritate me in various little ways. None of them serious. One Christmas he got drunk and that finished it for me. Frank was 10 years older than me. I'd been in danger of getting too deeply involved.

Frank didn't want to finish the relationship, but the end wasn't long in coming. One of the girls at work (they were never called anything else but girls, no matter how old they were) came and told me she'd seen him in the park "with that Elsie."

So that was it. Frank had obviously got the message and I was free again.

"Ernie's too bossy," Edie said. "Who does 'e think 'e is?"

"He's getting his feet under the table too much for my liking."

"I never could stand red hair."

"And his looks as if it's been cut with a lawn mower!"

Edie and I were suddenly pally trying to stick up for ourselves against Ernie. But he had made sure he was well in with father who seemed to let him do what he liked in the house. *Our* house!

"I'll bet they get married," Edie said.

"I hope they don't or they'll have to live here with us."

"That'll be nice, having him here all the time!"

Sure enough, a week or so later, Dolly and Ernie were engaged.

"I told you ..." Edie said in her infuriating way.

"Good job I didn't bet on it then.

"You'd have lost as usual."

When additional staff were taken on at B.A.T. their particulars came to us at the desk.

"St Edmund's College, eh!" The boss said, sounding impressed as he looked at the papers of one of the new girls, and this Mary was given a job with us at the desk.

"There's enough of us on desk work already," said Mr Jump,

one of the desk team. "Why's he bringing anyone else in to it?"

We soon found out. "Show Mary what's to be done," the boss told me. I did my best, covering up the mistakes she made. And that was my mistake! Trained by me, as soon as she'd begun to get a grasp of the job, I was out, back on the floor, while Mistress Mary took my place at the desk, which was pretty sickening.

The floor work had changed considerable during the months I'd been at the desk. The lay-out had been altered, new machinery installed. The long conveyor belts had gone. Now there were four of us to each machine. We fed the tobacco leaf into the machine which stripped away the stalk and dropped the leaves onto a small conveyor belt. One of the jobs was watching the conveyor belt carefully and picking out any leaf that had missed the stripping machine.

The horrible man I mentioned earlier was my boss now. I bumped into Alice, the girl I'd replaced on the desk. "So he did the same to you," she said.

"They told me you were leaving and that's how the vacancy at the desk came up."

"No, he's a right snob, that one. he decided you were a cut above me, right. And now he obviously thinks this new Mary's a cut above you."

Perhaps his conscience pricked him about this, because a few months later he promoted me to Section Hand.

"What does your father think about your promotion?" someone asked me.

"He doesn't know, I haven't told him." I never said much at home about work.

One of the big bosses came over from America to hold a meeting to tell us the bad news. Orders weren't coming in as they used to. It was the export market B.A.T. were interested in. Their cigarettes weren't sold over here at all. Snuff was made from the tobacco stems stripped away in our new machinery, but even this market was very poor. Snuff was beginning to go out of fashion.

A few days later it was announced we would be working half time and had to sign on the dole to make up our wages. On one visit to the Unemployment Office, one of the girls who was an only child, caused a sensation by wearing a coat down to her ankles. "It's the new look," she said proudly.

"It'll be ages before we can be in fashion," muttered Annie.

"Can you play tennis this afternoon?" Maggie asked me?

"I can , but I've only got one tennis ball ..."

"I'll try and get another from somewhere."

That's the way it was, Balls were expensive and nobody had more than two.

"OK. See you in the park."

"D'ye like the new look?"

"No. D'yu?"

"Can't see myself dressed up like that, somehow."

"I'm like that girl in the song — Miss Godet who wanted to die because she couldn't show her lovely legs."

"I'll be glad to cover mine up," I said. "But yours are nice."

"Thank you. Come on, we can have the court now."

She'd paid beforehand, sixpence each. When I got home, Dolly said, "It's all right for some, playing tennis instead of working."

"Nobody knows what you do at home all day."

"You can get the tea ready, go on!"

"Is Ernie coming?"

"Yes, we're getting engaged."

That shut me up. Dolly had thought it would be a nice little set-up, her with Ernie, me with Frank, but I wasn't having that.

"I'm not seeing Frank anymore." I told her.

"He was round yesterday, asking for you."

"Well, he needn't bother."

Edie came in. "Did you hear they're starting an Old Scholar's Guild? I'm not going."

A notice came round sating a meeting would be held in the school chaired by the ex-headmaster, Mr Hudson. It was arranged that there would be table tennis, snooker tables and various other facilities. The Guild was to be held once a week.

Once it got going, we all joined and found that 'Daddy Wat' was a really nice man now he had retired from school and was no longer the feared headmaster.

Once we were back at work full time, it didn't last long for some people. They started cutting down the workforce. It was a terrible blow, especially for those who were the sole breadwinners in the family. It began with late-comers, then it was just a random process, time-keeping cards were picked out from the clocking on machine and if your card came out, you'd had it.

They made their selection during the morning, so the first clue to your fate appeared at dinner time. If your card was missing from the slot, that was it. You knew your were finished. Your job was gone.

The Leeds Street factory finally closed. One of the bosses retired, the other took his place. The girls who knew him said, "he's strict, but he's fair." (which was more than anybody had ever said of Clough who'd gone by this time).

When he first came, he had a way of looking you in the eye when he was speaking to you, a piercing look. I made sure I stared straight back at him. He turned out to be my favourite. The girls used to tease me saying, "He's a bachelor you know. You'll be all right there!"

"It's not like that." I protested.

"Come on, we heard him this morning shouting, 'you're late Florence, you're late'. And then he clocked your card. He doesn't do that for anyone else does he?"

One time, when Ella and I were weighing ourselves after work, I put my foot on the scales to give her a bit of a shock, adding a few pounds just for a joke. Ella was very weight conscious. he came along just at that moment. I looked up at him and said, "It's all right, we're friends. I know her."

"Do you Florence? Have you lived with her then?"

"Yes, I have."

"Well, you do know her then, but have you no homes to go to?"

We went off home. He took a fatherly interest in me. He had a habit of leaning over a machine to tell you something or explain something, with his tie swinging about.

"He'll be catching it in the machinery one of these days," the girls used to say. And sure enough, that's what happened. His tie got caught in the machine and chewed up by it. He sent me out to be a new tie for him.

"How much did it cost?" they asked me. But I wasn't telling.

"I see the Corporation are building houses for rent," father said. "Though you'd probably need a letter from the Holy Ghost to get one."

"Some of the Councillors have moved in already," said Jack.

Dolly and Ernie were married and had two rooms in the house. I was sure they wouldn't be interested in a new house further away. It was more like their house than anybody else's.

Ernie'd say, "Don't you do that Doll, let them do it."

As though we weren't doing anything to help. As though we were treating the place like a hotel.

I'd been ill again. I'd been to another Convalescent Home in Wales. There were others there from work, convalescing. There was a woman who had been in the Dispatch Department who kept us amused with stories of how she'd driven lorries out of the factory during the strike, running the gauntlet of the picket line every time.

Chapter 20

When I returned to work, I'd lost the Section Hand's job on account of being away so much, and was moved to work on special leaf that had to be hand stemmed. There were only five girls on this work. One of them was Mary.

"How about coming to the Grafton Ballroom?" She asked me. "Wilf Hamer's band is there, and there's tea dances on a Saturday afternoon."

We went there together many times, except when the factory had a rush order and we had to work until four o'clock on the Saturday.

My friend Chrissie worked on a small cutting machine by herself. One day she chopped of the tops of two fingers. She spent all afternoon at the hospital being attended to. While she was away, two men came to fix a guard on the machine before the inspectors came to investigate the accident. She received no compensation, nothing but her sick pay from the Insurance Company.

I'd never been into the cutting room in the factory but one day I had occasion to go in there. Walking down the stairs to it, the sound of the cutting machines was loud, but inside the room itself, the noise was thunderous. Betty was with me.

"I thought the stemmery was bad," she said. "But this is

terrible."

"And they don't have ear-plugs or anything to protect them, do they, the people who work in here? It's enough to make you ill."

"No wonder they shout, even when they're working in other departments. Remember Vera that came to work with us? The boss was always telling her off for shouting."

At home these days, Dolly was completely taken up with Ernie. She had no time for anyone else.

Albert was not looking well. He didn't go out much. "How about a trip over the water on the ferry to Seacombe?" I suggested to him one day. "We could have a walk along the promenade to New Brighton."

He agreed, and we did this a few times. But gradually he found he couldn't walk that far. As the next stop for the ferry was Egremont, we tried that, but in the end we'd go straight to New Brighton just to sit on the pier and watch the ships passing or a cruiser anchored in the river waiting for the tug boats to guide it in to the landing stage. That was as much as Albert could manage. New Brighton was a very popular place then.

Unfortunately Albert was ill and had to go to Broadgreen Sanatorium. When we went to visit him, he said he'd like a watch. I bought him one.

Lily had come home from Broadgreen cured, but there was no cure for Albert. he died there, another victim of the dreaded consumption. With Alf, I'd never really believed he was dead. I always expected him to come home one day. But Albert's body was brought home so at least we had the comfort of seeing him in his coffin. He looked so pathetic lying there, so pale against ty purple silk lining. And younger than his 17 years.

The day of the funeral, Queenie came and cleaned and polished the house from top to bottom. Then something was said which offended one of them Dolly or Queenie, and they started a quarrel. The arrival of the undertaker put a stop to it.

After the funeral, the door was open for friends and neighbours coming back to the house. When Queenie arrived, Dolly slammed the door in her face. As everyone else came in, father asked, "Where's Queenie?"

"I don't know," said Dolly.

While I was still at home, Dolly sneaked out one day. "Where've you been?" I asked her

"To the hospital for Abbie's things."

"Why didn't you ask me to go with you?"

"I thought you'd be too upset."

Edie came home and said, "I see you've been for Abbie's things."

"Not me," I told her, repeating what Dolly had told me.

"I saw Ernie wearing Abbie's watch already."

"So that's why she didn't want me to go with her, then."

"You know what she's like."

So that was the end of that. It was no use saying anything to dad. In his eyes, Dolly could do no wrong.

The Old Scholar's Guild was going well, some of the teachers were keen too, which helped a lot. They supervised the play we were producing, for instance.

Discussing it on the way home and reminiscing about school days, Martha said, "Did you hear about Edith?"

"No, what about her?"

"She died."

"Oh no! How awful. Remember how she used to bring toast for us, for you and me?"

"Yes. I've never tasted toast as good again. Have you?"

"Trust you to remember the toast!"

"One of the lads was asking about you." Ben said.

"Which one?"

"That'd be tellin'"

"Don't be mean!"

"Well, if y're going to the park tomorrer night, he might be there."

Ella and I went to the park and met Stan and Ben. Walking home with them, as we reached the bottom of their road, Stan said, "Come in for a cuppa — the others have all gone out."

We went in the back way, a bit nervous as we had to pass an Alsatian dog tied up in the yard.

"It's all right, it won't touch you. It's wagging its tail."

"Yes, but that's not the end that bites!"

Stan made the tea and a sandwich. When he'd gone for the cups, we opened the sandwiches he'd given us. The meat was pieces of fatty ham. It was disgusting! We looked at each other and quickly slipped the ham into a handkerchief and fed it to the Alsatian on the way out.

"We never saw your admirer." Ella said.

"I wonder who it is. I don't remember any of them being in my class."

"They must look different now they're grown up. I wouldn't know. I didn't go to your school." And with that we went our separate ways.

After church on Sunday we usually went for a walk. We had a circular route that we followed, which brought us out on the main thoroughfare on the outskirts of Liverpool, Queens Drive. Somewhere in the middle of the walk we'd usually meet up with another group who had come the other way.

A few of the lads used to meet in a herb shop where they'd buy a drink of Vantas for a halfpenny. They always seemed to come out of the shop just as we were passing.

Which of them is it? I wondered. They were all friendly. When a dance was arranged, we had to persuade the boys to go. I'd seen this particular boy and liked the look of him. I was surprised to see him at the dance. There weren't any tables. You just put your coat in the cloakroom and, keeping hold of your handbag, found a corner where the group could congregate.

I'd only taken a purse with me. A handbag was a nuisance.

None of the boys wanted to keep an eye on a girl's handbag while she was dancing with one of the other fellows.

Now, getting up to dance, I asked this boy I found so attractive if he'd mind my purse. It was Stan I was having a dance with.

"What's his name?" I asked him.

"Who? This one who fancies you? That's Les. Les Jones."

"Is he any relation to David Jones, who used to sing with me when the Yanks were here?"

"He's David's brother."

The dance ws at Swainson, a popular cafe. In the interval Les asked, "D'ye want to go downstairs for refreshments?"

"Yes, I'd like that, thank you."

"Want anything to eat?"

"I'll have a chocolate biscuit please." I knew none of the lads had much money. but girls never paid for anything themselves anywhere.

Les was a long time coming back. "Been to Jacob's?" I asked.

"The place was packed."

"Just being friendly."

The only dance he did was the last waltz and then he took me home.

"Is it right you're Dave Jones' brother?"

"Yes, it is."

"Then you must be younger than he is." Younger than me.

"I am. I'm the youngest. I'm eighteen months younger than him. Does it matter?"

"Of course not. Some of my friends are younger than me."

Two of my best friends are younger than me. Three years younger. And we've been friends all our lives. Margery from our school days together and Elsie from work, from our time at the tobacco factory.

Lily and I had hoped to celebrate fifty years together, fifty years of friendship. But she didn't make it. She died of cancer. Poor Lily.

After the night of the dance, Leslie and I began to go out together. He went to night school three nights a week. he was studying for his City and Gilds certificate in joinery. So it was mostly a football match at the weekend we'd go to, and in the summer to New Brighton baths.

We were making arrangements to meet once when this chap came up to us and Les said, "this is my cousin, Charlie."

He asked us where we were going, and when we arrived at the baths, he was there waiting for us. "Thought I'd come and meet you here."

After the baths, Les came home with me for tea. I'd never done any cooking. A poached egg should be easy enough, I thought. It wasn't. After I'd broken three eggs, he came out to see what was taking so long.

"What's the cat eating?" he asked.

"It's all right now. They're broken."

"Good job they're cheap."

He never let me forget this incident!

Charlie found out where I worked and made it his business to be passing the house as I was coming out.

"I go your way," he said casually. "Might as well walk down together."

Suddenly however, Charlie's attentions stopped. I wondered why but never asked. Anyway, he was boring. It took him ages to say anything. He was too slow for me.

Although Les had been accepted at our house, I'd never been to his. "My mother wants you to come to tea on Sunday," he said one day. "She keeps saying she'd like to meet this girl who keeps me out so late." He usually got the last tram home at 11.45pm.

It was quite pleasant meeting the rest of his family. There were three brothers and one sister who always had her own way − until I joined them.

Dave was preparing for his wedding to Amy. The day of the wedding I was helping. "Will you take these up to the hall?" his mother said. She was doing all the catering for the wedding. When I got to the hall I was very surprised to see that his mother was there before me, although I'd only that minute left her in her own kitchen!

"You got here quickly." I said.

"I'm not Dave's mother," she said laughing. "I've been here a while. Everyone gets us mixed up."

They looked exactly the same to me. What a family that was. Les' father had many brothers and one sister named Olive. Les' sister was called after her Aunt Olive and some of the cousins were named Olive too. It was all very confusing. There were several Charlies too, and quite a few Williams. I don't think I ever sorted them all out.

Dolly decided it was too much for her, running the house, now she had a husband to look after.

"You'll have to leave work and take over," she said. "You're always ill anyway, you're always off sick. You'll be better off out of it."

I gave my notice in at work. The foreman I had crossed swords with said, "I hear you're leaving, then."

"Yes, I am."

"You're only going because Bill's leaving, aren't you?"

"Is he?" I didn't know that Bill was leaving.

"Yes, and I'm taking his place."

"that doesn't bother me, Mr Searle. You don't bother me."

"Then why're you going?"

"My health's not very good. You know that. Remember you had to take me home in an ambulance from the works' dance?

Remember?" It was the night I'd fainted and took such a long time to come round.

"I remember."

Mr Searle was the head of the St John's Ambulance Service at B.A.T. I didn't want him thinking I was afraid of him.

Nowadays, a few of us were spending the dinner hour in one or the other's houses. On Fridays we'd call in at a shop that sold lively meat pies. After she'd eaten her pie, this Winnie would always say, "Ooh."

"What's the matter?"

We knew what she'd say. It happened every week. "It's Friday isn't it. I shouldn't have eaten a meat pie. Now I'll haver to go to confession. Ooh!"

She never thought of this until after she's eaten her meat pie.

Did you hear about Margaret's mother?" mary asked.

We knew she'd been ill. "Is she worse?"

"She's dead, pour soul. They had an autopsy. And an inquest."

"Why?"

"Because they found arsenic in her hair."

It seems a friend had given her some pills she'd had from the doctor. "Heavens! That's dreadful! But why did she take someone else's medicine?"

"They both had the same complaint."

"It just shows people react differently to the same prescription."

None of us wanted to talk about it anymore.

"What did Searle say when he found out you were leaving?"

He thought it was because I couldn't face having him in charge of us."

"You would miss Mr R though, you can't deny it."

"Of course I would."

We made our way back to work. "I hope you'll still come to see me — wouldn't like to lose touch with you all."

"Of course we will, Flo."

I was strange not having to get up in the morning. Lying in bed while the other two were downstairs, Dolly cooking Ernie's breakfast and Edie doing her own. I waited to come down until they'd gone.

"There's some tea in the pot. I've just made it."

Once Dolly started to do anything, she started in the right way. "The man from the Co-Op comes for the grocery order," she said, giving me a list. "That's what I usually get."

The Co-Op man came and between them, he and Dolly made up the order. "You pay for it on Friday," he said.

This went on for a few weeks, with Dolly still deciding what was needed. They were so matey. I found out that I didn't like the man. But that wasn't unusual. I wasn't too keen on any of Dolly's friends. And the feeling was mutual — they didn't like me either!

"I'd rather have the Maypole margarine," I said. "And their jam is delicious, much nicer than the stuff from the Co-Op. Especially the Maypole strawberry jam. It's full of whole strawberries."

Apart from interfering in the weekly grocery order, Dolly didn't do anything to help me run the house. I had to fathom it out for myself. She had to use our cooker. Edie used to complain about the state Dolly left it in after she'd cooked Ernie's tea.

Still, I was happy looking after my little family. I felt comfortable and useful in my new domestic role. I felt I belonged there.

The only arguments in our house were about football, which was a common enough state of affairs, especially for families like ours living in the vicinity of rival football teams.

However, since Ernie had moved in with Dolly things had changed. Now we had frequent disagreements. He was a butcher and worked on Saturdays.

In between football seasons, Leslie's family went to Freshfield, a place with a sandy shore. Ten of us went together and while we played ball games, Mrs Jones sat and unpacked a picnic she'd brought for us all. She was a very good cook, Leslie's mother.

When we sat down to eat, somebody strummed on a banjo and afterwards we sang popular songs from the song sheets bought in Blackpool for a penny a time.

Leslie was serving his apprenticeship as a joiner and told some horrific tales of the places he had to visit. Some of the old slum courts had only one lavatory for so many families that it was in a frightful state. When the seat had to be replaced, for example, the joiner often couldn't bring himself to handle it and would just open the doors and throw in in.

Leslie had stated work at 14. At that time, he'd had to push hand-carts up the steep streets back to the carpenters shop where he worked.

Dockers would sometimes give him a push up the hill. "It's a disgrace," they'd say. "That poor lad pushing this heavy cart."

"You're right," others agreed. "It shouldn't be allowed."

Leslie had left school on the Friday and started work on the following Monday. His mother had made arrangements for him to work for a building contractor in a shop around the corner.

"I'm working my fingers to the bone," he'd complain to her. "While the boss' son just sits there twiddling his thumbs."

"You're getting paid."

"It's a dead-end job."

That was something I disagreed with his mother about. The same thing has been said to Leslie as had been said to me.

"Try to get into a drawing office," they'd said to him at school. And here he was working in the slums, replacing broken lavatory seats and rotting window frames, a long way from all his hopes.

Still, there was no choice. Like my family, his mother needed the money he brought home each week.

His mother was what you'd call a 'dyed in the wool' Conservative. She believed that people should stay in their place, stay in the station which the Good Lord had chosen for them.

She'd take me to the Conservative Party Socials and I'd sing for them. She knew nothing about politics, but staunchly defended any criticism of the Conservative Candidate at elections, and they always got round our way.

In spite of her political affiliations, Mrs Jones was a wonderful woman. Very caring. When my grumbling appendix finally had to be removed, she was the first visitor to the ward each night. This was a great comfort to me. I'd got used to nobody turning up until the visiting hour was nearly over.

I could forget about my own family now, about Dolly and Ernie, and Edie and Father. I seemed to have found myself a new family — Leslie's loving, caring family.

Chapter 21

Edie had this infuriating habit of borrowing my things. Going to a dance one night, I saw her there in the middle of the floor, wearing my dress.

"That's my dress you've got on!" I said, marching straight over to her. "It's a bit tight on you — you'll spoil it. In any case, I wanted to wear it myself. And you didn't even ask."

"Oh, don't go making a fuss, not here!"

"Why shouldn't I make a fuss, eh? Take my dress off. Take it off now!"

She didn't of course. At home, the row went on.

"You've ruined that one. And I don't know when I'll be able to afford another. You are a pig, Edie."

Money was scarce, especially now I wasn't working. And because of the depression, it was cash on the nail everywhere. No more tick, nothing on weekly payments.

"You've lent me dresses before."

"But you didn't ask, did you? Just sneaked out of the house in it. Hoping I wouldn't notice, no doubt. Anyway, you won't be able to wear my things much longer, you're getting fat, Edie." And with that I stalked off.

"Where are ye goin'?" she asked, running after me.

"Want to come?"

Our quarrel forgotten, we set off happily to see the postbox, where someone — someone Irish it was said — had left a bomb. The box was completely destroyed, shattered.

"Why do they do these things, the Irish?" we asked father later.

"They don't like the English. And they don't like the way the English have split their country in two, into North and South."

I'd read a book called Odd Man Out about a man in Ireland who'd planted a bomb. He'd been caught and shot, but somehow he'd managed to escape in spite of his wounds. He tried to find sanctuary, but nobody would risk sheltering him for fear of the consequences. How different it is in Ireland today.

"You shouldn't be hanging round such places," Leslie said when we told him. "My grandfather was an Orangeman and my father is one too. In fact, he's one of the leaders of the procession on the 12th July. Grandfather worked in the office of the Dock Board and he was told he was a marked man. He had to walk home through a hostile neighbourhood which made it worse."

"What did they mean by a 'marked man'?"

"The police had warned him he was on the list of the Sinn Fein. He'd be all right, he said. He had a gun."

"You won't use it will you, Mr Jones?"

"I certainly will, " grandfather is supposed to have said. "If I go down, five of them will go down with me."

Leslie's grandfather had died by this time, but the sons were all eager to tell stories about him. It was, however, only the eldest son – Leslie's father – who had followed in the old man's footsteps, but he never challenged the others.

Although Leslie had finished his apprenticeship, he still worked with the small contractor repairing run-down properties.

"You'll never be able to get married while you're with that firm," his brother Dave said to him. "Come and work with me. With your qualifications, your City and Guilds exam and all, you're wasted where you are."

So Leslie joined Dave. He was building new houses. Many private firms were building houses for sale and they were all in competition, so when one contract finished Dave and Leslie managed to move to another firm on another contract.

The best men were always able to find work, except for when they were 'rained off' and sent home without pay.

The money was good on these building projects. Seeking another job, the first question they were always asked was, "How much d'ye want?"

Their reply was always the same, "The Union rate." Although they were not in a union, they firmly agreed with the principal of no overtime while there were men out of work.

The Union Representative went round the building sites asking to see everyone's Union Cards, trying to catch out any employer paying 'under the lamp' – a popular way of describing poor pay. Eventually the Union Rep caught up with Leslie and Dave and they had to join the Union too.

The next question a prospective employer asked was, "How many doors can you hang in a day?"

If they said 11, they were told that with this firm they were expected to hang 12. Eventually the target reached 18. Each man had to do more than the next. It was a real cut-throat business.

Dave and Les soon earned reputations as good hard workers, and soon earned the nicknames 'Near Enough' (Dave) and 'Dead Level (Les) from the time they were working on a roof, one of them at either end, when this is what they called to one another as they erected the roof timbers.

"Near enough!"

"No, it must be dead level."

At work. Leslie was called George. At his christening and uncle had said, "Leslie! What sort of name is that? Give the lad a man's name, can't you. Suppose he goes to work at the docks?"

So he was George at work and Leslie at home!

On saturdays work on the building sites finished at midday. One Saturday, the row of houses they were working on still had no roofs on. As the weather forecast wasn't good, the boss asked the men to stay on and finish them.

The week before, a nearby building site had been left at the weekend with a row of roofless houses. On the Sunday a wind had sprung up and knocked the houses down like a pack of cards. Bearing this in mind, Dave, Leslie and a couple of others worked like slaves to get the houses finished, safe and sound against wind and rain. The four of them received a fiver between them for their trouble. One pound five shillings each — imagine!

Dave and Leslie had good reputations and weren't out of work much. Leslie was saving hard. I didn't have any money to save now that I wasn't working but running the house.

On that domestic front I was middling through. I hated cooking but had to do it. They ate what I put in front of them. Nobody complained. We had cookery books but they were only referred to for fancy things. I didn't even like the look of them.

And what was the point when we could buy the most beautiful doughnuts from the shop around the corner! Only threepence ha'penny for four, and so fresh that when you picked one up your fingers met in the middle and they really did melt in the mouth! Mmn, thinking of them today as I write makes my mouth water.

No, the recipe books weren't open very often in my kitchen. "Take six eggs ..." the recipe would usually begin. Cheap as eggs were, this seemed a frightful extravagance., especially as in my hands the end product would be scarcely recognisable as the light Victoria sponge in the recipe book.

Elizabeth Craig was not my favourite author!

I was still in the Concert Party. Leslie used to go with me although it was a bit boring for him. I even persuaded him to take charge of a coach full of kids on a Sunday School treat. The charabanc had gone by now.

Reluctantly he agreed. The children soon had him weighed up. They started throwing things out of the windows and then getting him to stop the coach so they could get them back off the road.

I had to take over. "The coach is not stopping until we get there," I said fiercely.

"Please Miss, can I get my handkerchief?" asked one girl. one of the ring-leaders.

"No. Why did you throw it out if you still wanted it?"

Leslie wasn't any happier on the way home. When we counted, one of the children was missing. "It's my mate's brother," he said. "What'll I do?"

"Go and check in the other coaches," I said.

And that's where the lad was, on one of the other coaches with his mates.

"Never again!" said Les. "Never again!"

Edie had a boyfriend now. He was all right except that he went drinking with the rest of them. We didn't, Les and I. Neither of the men were keen on football, Edie's nor Dolly's. Both were butchers which meant they worked on Saturdays when the football matches were played.

When our dog died, Leslie bought me a Scotch Terrier which I called Angus. We'd always had mongrels before.

Outside Dolly's rooms along a small passage was a butler's pantry with a wide shelf. It was at the top of the cellar steps. Dolly was out one day when Ernie sent the meat round from the shop. I took it in and put it on this shelf. A bit later on while I was downstairs, I heard the dog growling. It was pulling at something from under the dresser. It was Dolly's steak!

The cat had jumped on the shelf and knocked the parcel downstairs, and dragged it under the dresser. I managed to rescue the meat and wiped it over and put it back on the shelf just as Dolly came in.

"Your steak's there," I said.

"Did you enjoy your dinner?" I asked her later.

"Yes, the steak was very tender."

"I thought it would be."

"Why d'ye ask?"

"Just that the cat and the dog had a tug of war with it."

"Why didn't yeh tell me?"

"You enjoyed it didn't you? It hasn't done you any harm."

Father had a hernia and wore a truss. He was in his sixties and too old for an operation, they said. He still kept a close eye on our manners. When we were going out it was, "Fasten your coat and put your gloves on before you go."

Dolly often used to sulk. Sometimes I was quite bewildered, not knowing what had upset her. Then it was awful until Edie came home.

"What's up with 'er today?"

"I don't know."

I met a friend one day who said, "Your Dolly's renting a house a few doors away from where you used to live."

"She hasn't told us."

The next day, a furniture van drew up outside the house. "It's for me," Dolly said.

"You might have told us. Why are you going?"

"You're getting married, and I can't live with Edie."

I told Edie that when she came home.

"I know why she's going," she said. "I've been telling her off for using your eggs and bacon in the morning."

"I've been thinking they were disappearing quickly, the groceries."

Dolly didn't have much more to do with us after that. I was finding the going very hard. For me, reading was the only pleasure left at home.

Edie and I often disagreed, but we never sulked. Of course, she was still favourite with dad, but it was better without Dolly and Ernie. Before long, Dolly had a baby and we went to see her, but we were not made welcome.

"I'm not bothering with her any more," said Edie. "She doesn't want anything to do with us, that's obvious."

Lily married a man she'd met in the sanatorium. At the wedding, Dolly was in the church. "We should speak to her," I said to Edie.

"You can, I'm not going to."

I went over and spoke to her but she ignored me.

"I told you," Edie said.

"I'm still wondering what I'd done to offend Dolly.

"Are you playing tennis again?"

"Yes, Edie. As I'm carrying a racquet that's what I'm gong to do."

"Any luck with the house yet?"

"No. I only want a new one. One without creepy crawlies."

"They don't bother me."

Les and I had been trying to find a house to rent, but it looked as though we'd have to buy one. Leslie applied for a mortgage and we chose a house on the estate where he was working. We had nobody to advise us but we managed on our own, and as soon as we were married, we moved into our brand new home.

Father came down a few times. "It's a bit small, isn't it?" he said the first time he saw it, which was ridiculous considering they'd brought up seven children in a house with smaller rooms and no bathroom.

After Edie was married, father went to live with Dolly, and after Marion's christening, never came to visit us again.

Edie and I saw each other once a week. She and Tommy were married a few months after us. They lived over the butcher's shop.

Father was 94 when he died. Dolly didn't let any of us know. It was after the funeral that we heard he was dead when a friend showed us the death's column in the paper.

"What about insurance policies?" she asked. "Didn't you all have to sign?"

Evidently not. Nobody had contacted either of us about father's insurance policy. "Typical Dolly," Edie and I agreed.

Years later, I bumped into a neighbour who used to live near us in Verona Street. "By the way, did you see the Echo last night?" she asked me.

"No, why?"

"There's a picture of your sister in it," she said as she hurried on her way.

I bought the paper. In the centre page there was a picture of Dolly sitting among the rubble of Verona Street. The houses had all been knocked down, but the paper said she was refusing to leave.

"She's still as stubborn as ever then," I said to Edie later.

"Seems like it."

She looked stupid in the picture. And she had to move out in the end. But that was the last we saw of her. After that, Dolly just seemed to drop out of existence.

Chapter 22

During the five years we were engaged, more of Leslie's relations seemed to turn up everywhere. "There's my uncle," Leslie said, pointing out a man with a white beard.

"Oh yes, of course," I answered, which was the in thing for us to say if we saw anybody looking different.

We were on holiday in North Wales and his mother was with us. She introduced us to this man, "My brother in law."

"So he really is your uncle," I said, feeling embarrassed because I hadn't believed him. "How many more have you got?"

Queens Drive Baths decided to have mixed bathing although one sex had to climb out of the water on their own side, no one dared do otherwise.

In 1937 after being engaged for five years Leslie put down a deposit on a house on the estate where he had been working and we were married. A friend who'd been married a few moths earlier lent me her wedding dress. Edie got married three months later and went to live over the butcher's shop where Tommy worked, still in the neighbourhood.

"You'll be miles away," Edie said. "I wouldn't like to live right out there."

"Nobody's asking you to."

It wasn't too far for Ella and Lily to come and visit.

I knew nothing about the facts of life. When I was pregnant, Lily had to tell me. Leslie's mother never talked about anything like that. It was only when I met a friend from work who told me what to do that I went to hospital.

When the baby came I had a terrible time and it took me years to recover properly. I was told by the Ward Sister not to have any more children as I wasn't made for childbirth.

The first day, non-family were allowed in, some of them meeting for the first time since the wedding. As I was on the balcony, the hospital rule of two visitors per bed was waived.

As Leslie's family poured in exchanging news and greetings, I lay there watching them talking away to each other and ignoring the one they'd come to see!

In those days, hospitals were places to avoid if possible, like the dentist. The nurses were like slaves, keeping the place tidy. Once a week, the ward was cleaned, the beds pulled out from the walls with a dragon of a Sister supervising. The Matron, a terrifying figure, visited each ward once a week and stood at the end of each ed and asked, "How are you?"

What could anyone say except, "Fine, thank you."

When the doctors cam round no patient dared to speak to them. We were all tucked in neatly like so many parcels and identified only by our bed numbers. The doctors themselves were treated like little tin gods.

The news in the papers and wireless was very disturbing. News of the atrocities carried out by the Germans.

The talk everywhere was of war. "Not again," father said when we were visiting him one day. "It's not so long after the last one."

"We've bought a wireless set."

"A new one?"

"No, it was 15 shillings second hand." (75p in today's money).

"What about the Zeppelin flying over the Mersey then?"

"It was supposed to have lost its way."

"It was flying so low, you could see the name on it, The Hindenburg."

"They say it flew right the way over the docks. You mark my words, we'll soon be at war with Germany."

Home from the hospital, I'd lost about two stones in weight. Neither of us knew anything about looking after a baby, but we coped. And his work was only a few minutes away, so that was a help.

When I was ill, my next door neighbour, Sal, often took Marion for a few hours to give me a break. After such a difficult birth, I couldn't believe the baby was all right. I became quite neurotic, and took her to the doctor for the least little thing.

he didn't mind because there was no National Health Service then we had to pay. When I had to be out for any length of time, I'd leave her with my mother in law who'd had five children of her own, but even then, I always hurried home in case anything had happened to the baby.

When Marion was 12 months old, the rumours of war became reality. World War II has started — England was at war with Germany.

Immediately, all house building stopped except for an estate of Corporation houses which hadn't yet been allocated to tenants. The Government took these houses over and they were altered for the soldiers of the Pioneer Corps to live in. Later, Italian Internees lived in them.

Every eligible male had to be interviewed for the Armed Forces. Some were conscripted, whilst others like Leslie were sent to the docks to prepare the troop ships.

All women over 18 were interviewed for war work but those with babies were left at home. Many women were sent to jobs that they hated, jobs for which they were entirely unsuitable. Manual work, say for someone who was not used to that sort of thing.

Some joined up for the Land Army. Edie was pregnant so she didn't have to take war work. Her husband was in the Territorial Army and was sent to some remote place in England.

With Les working miles away and all the hours God sends, our quiet life was shattered. Sometimes he'd be working all night and come home and drop into bed exhausted.

My life seemed to be all standing in queues. After waiting hours for our ratio books, we had to queue for meat, sausages if we were lucky.

Now and then word would go round that the fruit shop had

bananas in. Sometimes we'd be lucky and get one after waiting an hour in the queue, but as often as not, by the time we reached the counter the bananas had gone. But it didn't put us off next time. Imagine queuing in a shop for an hour in the hope of getting a banana. One banana!

When the air raids started, it came as a shock, going down town and seeing the devastation caused by the bombing the night before. We were lucky to be living in the suburbs. Every night, people trailed down in droves to escape from the city and the bombing.

We all huddled in shelters. Sometimes ours was flooded and it was difficult to find a way of keeping our feet dry as we perched on the bunks in the darkness.

We became used to the sound of the double buzz from the engines of the German bombers hovering overhead. At this stage, we had no notion of the horrors that were to come.

As a little girl I'd enjoyed the First War. I'd enjoyed the Americans, the concerts. It wasn't until afterwards that I learned about the suffering. Now it was a war for civilians. 20 years of uneasy peace had been shattered and now we faced six years of bitter war.

And after this war, life would never be the same again.

Temperance Poem

A Teetotal Doll

My friends, it's very sad I think
When even dollies take to drink
The specimen tonight you've seen
Will show how dreadful she has been.

My doll is here for you to see
I'll tell you she's quite TT
She's never touched a drop of drink
And so far keeps far from ruin's brink.

I ask all the parents here tonight
To sign the pledge, the drink to fight
Example to your children give
Teach for eternity to live.

Temperance Song

Gay Venetian Gondoliers we
From a southern land kissed by the sun.
As the hours pass by our Gondoliers ply
'Neath the bridges we pass one by one.

'Tis a task that is pleasant to do
But the best time of all is at night
When the moon rises high in the beautiful sky
And we glide in a glorious light.

... chorus ...

In a gondola, in a gondola, on the dark canal
Brightest come moons in Venetian skies
Visions entrancing to mortal eyes

In a gondola, in a gondola, 'tis a lovely sight
A pathway of silver that ripples
And moves in the pale moonlight.

Seems to me as we glide along
There is purity breathed by the air
And the water so clear is our hearts most dear
And to drink far away drives dull care

Here's a lesson to all who are sad
And through drink are inclined to lose heart
Out the chain and be free, be as happy as we
From the toils of king alcohol part

... *chorus* ...

In a gondola, in a gondola,
'Tis a lovely sight
There's no drink like water
To make the head clear
And a heart keep light.

Eclipse

"You'll see it better in the park"
My father said.
"A total eclipse of the sun
May be seen here once in a lifetime."
So I joined the people in the park,
A laughing, happy crowd
Looking up into the sky
Through pieces of coloured glass.

As the moon crept between sun and earth
There came a stillness, strange and awesome
No wind, no shadows, no birds singing
Only cold darkness, a dog howling mornfully.

Gradually the sun emerged
Turning bushes and trees into ghostly shapes
Some fell to their knees and prayed
While others said —
"No wonder the sun was once a God
For how could we live without it?"

F. Jones

Tailpiece

Florence is 85 years old now. She and Les still live in the newly built house they bought before the last war and their daughter, Marion, is a Registrar in Brougham Terrace.

Despite her advancing years, Florence is still a member of the local writers' club. She regularly sends letters to popular magazines — which are often published, and enters many competitions.

She still has plenty of fascinating stories to tell about her life, and feels that, if God is merciful, she may share them in the near future ...